MARY STU, ...

Friedrich Schiller

MARY STUART

a new adaptation by Robert Icke

OBERON BOOKS
LONDON

WWW.OBERONBOOKS.COM

First published in 2016 by Oberon Books Ltd
521 Caledonian Road, London N7 9RH
Tel: +44 (0) 20 7607 3637 / Fax: +44 (0) 20 7607 3629
e-mail: info@oberonbooks.com
www.oberonbooks.com

PB ISBN: 9781786820259
E ISBN: 9781786820266

Cover design: James Illman

Printed and bound by 4edge Limited, Essex, UK.
eBook conversion by CPI Group (UK) Ltd, Croydon, CR0 4YY.

Visit www.oberonbooks.com to read more about all our books and
to buy them. You will also find features, author interviews and news
of any author events, and you can sign up for e-newsletters so that
you're always first to hear about our new releases.

'Tell all the Truth but tell it slant'

Emily Dickinson

'The persona is a complicated system of relations between the individual consciousness and society, fittingly enough a kind of mask, designed on the one hand to make a definite impression upon others, and, on the other, to conceal the true nature of the individual... 'High rests on low' says Lao-tzu. An opposite forces its way up from inside.'

Carl Jung, *Two Essays on Analytical Psychology*

'It was Wilson; but now it was my own voice I heard, as he said: "I have lost. Yet from now on you are also dead... In me you lived – and in my death – see by this face, which is your own, how wholly, how completely, you have killed – yourself!"'

Edgar Allan Poe, *The Story of William Wilson*

"Women have one of the great acts of all time. The smart ones act very feminine and needy, but inside they are real killers... There's nothing I love more than women, but they're really a lot different than portrayed. They are far worse than men, far more aggressive, and boy, can they be smart."

Donald Trump, *The Art of the Comeback*

Nothing terrifies actors like verse. Verse often means Shakespeare, and Shakespeare means rules. Right ways and wrong ways. But there aren't any rules – at least, none that Shakespeare himself ever thought worth setting down.

It's sometimes unclear quite what people mean when they comment on verse being 'well spoken' or on 'good verse speaking' – what they often mean is that the language is being spoken in a different kind of voice (posher and louder, usually) or explained (as if talking to a class of children, or to someone hard of hearing).

A century ago in England, verse-speaking meant speech as song: sonorous vocal effects drowning the nuance and detail of meaning. The next wave was an academic sharpness – meaning and sense – but with a pedantic focus on setting the rules of verse, and on the pointed underlining of literary terms (most of which were invented long after Shakespeare's death), iambic pentameter, caesura, antithesis and so on. The fallout from these ideas have badly damaged actors' relationship to Shakespeare in the English-speaking world – none more disastrously than the idea that every line of verse should finish with a pause.

In the meantime, American writers took the richer, organic, essential inheritance of Shakespeare: Kushner, Albee and Sorkin, to name but three, write words in music, in rhythm. Dialogue is musical.

Words are sound and sense – and not just sense. And sound and sense cannot be separated. Words built up into sentences have rhythm when spoken aloud. And verse (that is, a regular rhythmic structure underneath a sentence) can add pressure and petrol and poise to a thought. Verse is thought blossoming, bursting into words – in real time.

You should no more be aware of verse spoken than someone listening to music is aware of the beats of the bar. Or any more aware than you are of the number of vowels in this sentence. They're there, certainly, but they do not contain its deepest (or even shallowest) meanings. They are part of its meaning, part of its structure – but the number of them, the flow of them and their totality is difficult to describe. But you can kind of feel it. There's shape and architecture, swooping, soaring, sometimes hesitant *rhythm.*

Verse is a way of allowing energy into the sense of a line through its sound. It allows variety, and allows it in several ways: by allowing the first or last or middle word of a line to shake its rhythm, in the cumulative energy as the items in a list mount up on top of each other, or in the crisp, hard facts of monosyllables.

The heartbeat of an iamb closely echoes the human heartbeat. A continuing rhythm, like the bassline in a piece of jazz, and one that gives life. It gives no instruction to the actor. It is not to be counted or observed – though also not to be ignored. Hamlet warns us that – like all great art – it's a matter of balance: discretion and also wildness ('too tame' is deadly).

The verse is the structure of the pipe. The words are the water. The pressure of the jet of water is a combination of the two things. The sound and the sense are two sides of the same coin. Inseparable, neither could exist without the other; and mutually enriching.

The fact that there are five iambs in a line is a fact comparable to the fact that there are sixty seconds in a minute. It's not that the minute pauses after the sixtieth. It's not that we notice (or would want to notice) every time a second ticks from 'sixty' back round to 'one'. It's just an underlying structure, and one our lives sometimes observe (when, for example, the news begins exactly on the hour), sometimes not (at exactly what time did you go to bed last night?).

The seconds beat quickly through the minute. The minutes beat slower, deeper, through the hour. Your life plays out messily on top of that structure – is playing out right now across that structure, even as you read this – living through that structure and with it and despite it. The beat is everywhere. Each life finding its own way through it, its own form and speed and flow. There really aren't any rules.

RI
November 2016

Acknowledgements

I am indebted and grateful to all of the actors who read the play on the page, in a workshop reading, or in the rehearsal room for their time and their thoughts – and additionally to Rupert Goold, Josh Higgott, Julia Horan, Laura Marling, Lucy Pattison, Emma Pritchard, Ilinca Radulian, Daniel Raggett – and last (and most) Zara Tempest-Walters.

It's a play. It isn't history.

This adaptation of Friedrich Schiller's MARIA STUART (1800) was written to be produced in contemporary or timeless costume, not in the clothes of either Elizabethan England or Schiller's Germany. That is, the setting is 1587; the time is now.

Though Schiller consulted numerous historical sources, much of his play – including the character of Mortimer, and the queens' meeting – has no basis in historical fact. This version makes some cuts, partly for length, partly for leanness, and partly to enable a cast size of twelve. This text has four further handmaidens in the final act, but their lines are easy to cut, and Mary could certainly bequeath her belongings to absent handmaidens (via Melvil) should future productions so desire.

It is usually assumed that Schiller's first act takes place on one day, a month after Mary's trial, that the second, third and fourth act all occur on a second (the same) day, and then the fifth act on a third day. In this version, the action is compressed still further: to occur in a single (slightly more than) twenty-four hour period, beginning in the morning of one day and moving through to Mary's execution before dawn on a second. Elizabeth's final scene occurs at some point later on the second day.

Schiller either didn't know or didn't care that the travel between Fotheringay and London would take much longer than his play allowed – and almost certainly knew that this structure played fast and loose with historical events and their sequence. But then his design is symmetrical, not historical. The first and fifth acts are Mary in prison, the second and fourth Elizabeth at court, and in the third and central act, the two queens meet in the open air. The play's final scene sits outside of this mirrored structure – as if a new play is beginning now the old one's great rivalry has been ended.

Again: it isn't history.

The first production had two actors learn the roles of both queens, and, by spinning a coin live at the beginning of the evening, randomly determine which queen would be in power and which in prison – lending a play constructed around doubles, mirrors, equivalences, differences and mighty opposites a formal duality all of its own. It also allowed the first word of the evening to anticipate its ending: 'Heads'.

Characters

MARY STUART, the exiled Queen of Scotland

Hanna KENNEDY – her servant

MELVIL – her chief of staff

QUEEN ELIZABETH I, Queen of England

Sir Amias PAULET – Mary's current jailer

MORTIMER – his nephew

William Cecil, Lord BURLEIGH

Lord George TALBOT, Earl of Shrewsbury, Mary's former jailer

Robert Dudley, Earl of LEICESTER

Lord AUBESPINE, the French ambassador

William DAVISON, Elizabeth's secretary

Henry Grey, Earl of KENT

and Mary's ladies in waiting ALIX, GERTRUDE, MARGARET & ROSALIND

This adaptation was commissioned by and originally produced at the Almeida Theatre, where it had its first performance on 2 December 2016.

Cast (in alphabetical order)

Aubespine	Alexander Cobb
Mortimer	Rudi Dharmalingam
Burleigh	Vincent Franklin
Davison	David Jonsson
Leicester	John Light
Kennedy	Carmen Munroe
Melvil	Eileen Nicholas
Kent	Daniel Rabin
Paulet	Sule Rimi
Mary Stuart/Elizabeth I	Juliet Stevenson
Talbot	Alan Williams
Mary Stuart/Elizabeth I	Lia Williams

Creative Team

Direction	Robert Icke
Set and Costume Design	Hildegard Bechtler
Composition	Laura Marling
Lighting	Jackie Shemesh
Sound	Paul Arditti
Video	Tim Reid
Casting	Julia Horan CDG
Associate Director	Daniel Raggett
Resident Director	Ilinca Radulian

The show then transferred to the Duke of York's Theatre, West End, where it had its first performance on 13 January 2018, where it played with the following cast changes:

Cast

Talbot	Michael Byrne
Paulet	Christopher Colquhoun
Aubespine	Calum Finlay
Burleigh	Elliot Levey

A note on the text

A forward slash (/) marks the point of interruption of overlapping dialogue.

A comma on a separate line (,) indicates a pause, a rest, a silence, an upbeat or a lift. Length and intensity are context dependent.

Square brackets [like this] indicate words which are part of the intention of the line but which are *not* spoken aloud.

This text is written to be spoken fast.

ACT ONE

A room in a prison in the Castle of Fotheringay. HANNA KENNEDY (elderly, quietly ferocious, fiercely loyal) is mid-argument with SIR AMIAS PAULET. MORTIMER (young, intense, unflinching eyes) is searching the room.

PAULET   This is a jewel –

KENNEDY   It isn't yours to take

PAULET   A jewel – you can't deny it when it's in my hand

KENNEDY   Paulet, you've searched this place

PAULET   And found a *jewel*

KENNEDY   You found it in the grass, not up in here –

PAULET   – and jewels don't grow on trees. This thing was *thrown*
            Thrown from the window for someone to find –
            A bribe. A payment. Who knows what it means?
            I haven't slept, I've watched and watched and watched
            and *still* you lying women slip things through
            still some hidden dangers here to find –

MORTIMER finds a hidden stash of letters. KENNEDY is incriminated, angered.

KENNEDY   LEAVE THOSE ALONE
            Her secrets are not yours

PAULET   Once they are found, they are

KENNEDY   She writes things down – it's just to pass the time
            They're drafts of letters to the Queen of England –

PAULET   Then I'll deliver them.

KENNEDY   Please – don't take those – you've stolen *everything*

PAULET   We'll store them with the other things we found.
            We'll keep them safe. In time, you'll get them back.

MORTIMER exits. PAULET looks at KENNEDY.

KENNEDY   What you are doing to us is outrageous.
Who would look at these bare walls and say
'A *Queen* lives here'? Where is the throne?
Where are her golden canopies of state?
There is no mirror here / for her

PAULET   it isn't safe

KENNEDY   You took her books –

PAULET   I said: it isn't safe

KENNEDY   Tell me when *music* became dangerous

PAULET makes the case, spelling it out:

PAULET   While she owns things, the country isn't safe
Look, it's a weapon if it's in her hands.

,

KENNEDY   A queen is not a common criminal

PAULET   A criminal is not commonly a queen.

KENNEDY   Your prisoner, Paulet – she was born a queen
She was a queen when she was six days old,
Raised in soft beds. She *is not used to this.*
It should have been enough to take her power:
But little things that keep someone *alive* –
please – be kind – don't be the man who takes
the last few things that decorate our life
they're all that's left

PAULET   Distractions will not help her to repent
or make atonement for the life she's led

KENNEDY   If in her younger years she made mistakes
then she answers to God – and her own heart
There is no judge in England over her

PAULET   She'll get her judgement where she broke the law

KENNEDY   How can she break the law from this bare cell?

PAULET   But yet – from a bare cell, her arm stretched out
            into the world – a sequence of attacks
            beat at the doors of our safety –
            and strangely, every time it looked the same:
            they'd kill the Queen,
            and install Mary on the English throne
            so first the Duke of Norfolk tried his luck
            plotted to murder God's anointed Queen
            he failed, then William Parry whet his knife
            he was, I think, a friend of Mary's, he
            attempted to assassinate the Queen –
            then, somehow, from her cell, Lady Mary Stuart
            got letters out to Babington, lit *his* flame,
            (I don't know *how* she did it but she did)
            incited *him* to regicide – which he tried
            and failed – and died. Norfolk, William Parry, Babington
            all dead – all lost their lives – for Mary's sake.
            Three noble heads cut off in sacrifice
            For her. But nothing – *nothing* – can deter
            the jostling swarms of madmen, pushing forth
            to jump into the abyss – to waste their lives – *for her.*
            And every day the scaffolds heave to hang
            the new – and newer – martyrs for her cause.
            Black day that England ever welcomed her.

KENNEDY   Did England *welcome* her? Since that black day
            when she, a queen, set foot on England's soil
            to ask her cousin – fellow queen – for help –
            despite her royal prerogative – she has
            (against all international laws) been locked in here
            in prison. She came here as a refugee –

PAULET   She came here as a murderer on the run
            from her own people, exiled from a throne
            that she'd contaminated with her sordid crimes
            She came here to restore the Catholic faith
            She came here to usurp the rightful Queen.

KENNEDY   That's just not true –

PAULET   Then why won't she renounce her claim?

          ,

Why not just say – in public – that she has
no claim, no hope of being England's queen?
But she won't do it. She could sign her name
on that one document – and she'd walk free.
But no, she won't. And why won't she? Because
she still intends – she still has hope – with sleight
and skill and secret, violent plots
to conquer England from her prison cell.

KENNEDY   You're joking – you have to be [joking] –
these hopes you say she has – she's *in a cell,*
no voice of comfort, no sight of her friends
only these men who stare into her cage

PAULET   No cage protects us from her evil brain
How do I know the bars have not been filed?
or that these walls and floor aren't hollowed out
for treachery to tunnel in at night?
I wish your devil queen was somewhere else.
I wish I'd never taken up this post –
I just can't *sleep,* I check and check and check
the locks, the doors, the walls – I wake up *cold*
my dreams like needles – she's sneaked something through
and a slip of my mind is a slip of the locks
and all my men lie lifeless on the stone
and Mary's next attack is hurtling forth –

    MARY enters.

KENNEDY   My lady, they are crushing us –

MARY   Be calm
Tell me, Hanna – what has happened now?

KENNEDY   They took your letters – and your marriage jewels,
the things we kept, the last few things we saved
He's got them all. There's nothing royal left.

MARY   Compose yourself.
              These outward trappings do not make the queen.
              They have the power to treat us basely, but
              They cannot debase us. In England, I have learned
              to let things go. And this: just one more thing.
(To PAULET.) You're holding something there I'd hoped to give you:
              among those papers, one is for your Queen,
              a letter to my royal sister – give me your word
              that you'll deliver it – place it in *her* hand

PAULET   I'll do what I think best.

MARY   Sir, all it says [is this] –
              the letter asks her for a great favour –
              I ask her for an audience in person –
              We've never met. I've never seen her face.
              The men that judged me – they were not my peers
              no man in England shares my royal birth
              I can't accept their judgement of my case
              My *only* equal is Elizabeth:
              my only equal breathing England's air.
              Your Queen alone is of my blood – my sex
              to her alone – as sister, queen and woman
              can I speak freely

PAULET   You've opened up your heart before to men
              who were less worthy of your royal trust

MARY   I ask her for a second favour, one
              inhuman to refuse: she took my crown
              my freedom and my life from me –
              perhaps my head is next – but not my soul
              she cannot want my soul, and for some time
              I have been asking for my basic right:
              I wish to practise *my* religion –

PAULET   Whenever you like, the Dean / of the prison

MARY   I have nothing to say to the Dean. A priest
              of my own church is what I'm asking for
              (as you well know). My days are numbered now.
              I'm waiting for my death –

21

PAULET   at least you know

MARY   – and I want to write a will.

PAULET   Go right ahead.
              The Queen desires no profit from your things.

MARY   And where are my women? I was separated
              from them – it's not that I need maids – it's just
              I want to know that they're alive and well

PAULET   They are. They're fine.

MARY   Are you leaving?

              ,

              Before you do, you could at least release
              my heart from its uncertainty. You see,
              in prison, you have me confined. No news
              gets through. This prison is my world.
              It's been a month – and a long month – since I
              was taken by surprise by forty men,
              commissioners, who rushed into this prison
              and set up court, completely unannounced,
              I had no lawyer – but they made me answer
              their formal charges – their words bristling with traps
              I was in shock, could barely speak, but I
              from memory replied as best I could –
              then, like ghosts, they were gone. Since that day
              nothing. Silence.
              Now, I look into your eyes – is my fate there?
              Who won the vote? My friends – or enemies?
              And should I live in fear – or live in hope?

              ,

PAULET   Settle your account with heaven.

MARY   I pray to heaven for mercy – but on Earth
              I pray for justice.

PAULET   Oh, it's coming, don't worry –

MARY Have they reached a verdict?

PAULET   I don't know.

MARY Look: *is* my sentence death?

PAULET   I just don't know

MARY Things happen fast in England. Like my trial.
I'm sure my murder will be just the same:
no warning.
But then what's left that could surprise me now?
That they think they can judge me! – but I know
the depths to which your Queen's not scared to sink,
the darker moves Elizabeth dares make –

PAULET The Crown of England has no fear at all,
outside its conscience and its Parliament.

Enter MORTIMER, swiftly. He's young, seems strict.

He pointedly (and entirely) ignores MARY.

MORTIMER Uncle, they're looking for you.

Exit MORTIMER. MARY catches PAULET as he makes to follow.

MARY Let me just say – you *do* have my respect
I know this situation tests you too
and anything *you* have to say to me, I'll listen
But keep that boy away from me – your nephew:
his arrogance is more than I will bear.

PAULET And that's exactly why he's valuable.
He travelled, went to Paris, and to Rheims,
and came back just as English as he left.
Your crocodile tears won't melt his heart.

PAULET exits.

KENNEDY That he *dares* speak like that – to you –
and to your face – it's hard for me to hear

MARY is lost in thought.

MARY   When we were in our former radiance
we listened only to the flatterers;
it's justice: now we only hear contempt
it's a lesson, Hanna.

KENNEDY   hey – my sweetheart, we are not defeated
Now – where's the girl who used to comfort me?
It was your fickleness I had to tell you off for,
Much more than gloom –

MARY   You've forgotten, Hanna,
what today is. The anniversary of Darnley's death
another black mark on the calendar.
at night, his milky eyes still stare at me
face dashed with blood – He'll never let me sleep.

KENNEDY   Forgiveness has been granted by the Church

MARY   No priest has ever laid that ghost to rest – or penance / either

KENNEDY   You *did not murder him* – your hands were clean

MARY   'My hands were clean' – my *conscience* isn't clean.
Yes, Bothwell murdered Darnley, but *I knew.*
and driven by my lust – a deadly sin –
I married Darnley (sin) gave him a crown
(another sin: defiling my own throne)
then gave my heart to Bothwell – (sin sin sin)
and pulled a world of guilt down on myself

KENNEDY   My sweetheart, why dig up your history?
You were so young –

MARY   I hated Darnley, wanted a divorce
wanted him gone so I could get to Bothwell
but God in heaven knows how hard, how *far*
I fell for *him* – I was his prisoner – anything he asked –
and Darnley's life was nothing to me, then –

KENNEDY   Falling in love's a madness with no cure
but time. Bothwell was evil to the bone.

MARY   It's my own weakness – weak before the men –

KENNEDY Some shameless demon screamed inside you too:
you wouldn't hear the warnings, you were *blind*
possessed – I couldn't believe you were still you,
parading Bothwell through the streets of Edinburgh
(and not ashamed that people knew the truth:
that a murderer was the lover of the queen)
you made his judges clear him of his crime –
and then – oh God

MARY   don't stop – I married him.

,

I think back – I don't recognise myself.

KENNEDY I know you. Who you are. You're gentle. Open.
You won't be damned for that. You do feel shame.
I nursed you, I should know – so be at peace.
Everyone has history they'd rather forget.
Whatever else you are, you're innocent *here*
in *England* there's no sin you're guilty of –
and England's Parliament is not your judge.
The only thing that holds you here is force.

*Enter MORTIMER, fast. The two women are shocked. Could this be
the feared assassination? As MORTIMER produces a letter, MARY
flinches as if it might be a knife – as he speaks urgently to KENNEDY.*

MORTIMER Get out there. Guard the door.
I need to speak with the Queen.

MARY   No, Hanna, stay –

MORTIMER Don't be afraid.

MORTIMER hands MARY the letter. She opens it, fearful –

MARY   And what is [this] – ?

She's looked at it, stunned. MORTIMER turns to KENNEDY again.

MORTIMER Wait outside. My uncle's coming. Please.
We don't have long.

MARY   Go! Go! Do what he says –

KENNEDY, surprised, leaves.

It's from my uncle, the Cardinal of Lorraine

MORTIMER nods: she's understood something. She reads the letter:

'trust Mortimer, the bearer of this letter: there's
no friend more loyal to you in all the world'.

Can this be true?

MORTIMER Forgive the way I was – it was a mask,
the only way to get to you – the only way
to bring you help – and rescue

MARY   I'm in shock
I can't believe there's hope – so fast – I've been in prison
now for [so long] – sir, please explain yourself

MORTIMER Your Majesty, time is short. My uncle's coming back.
The man he's bringing with him hates you –
and once they're here, given that [sentence is passed] – but first
let me start by – I'm sorry. It's seeing you.
I don't – it's seeing you in person.

MARY   *Please* – explain

MORTIMER I have been raised a Protestant – as a child
they taught me to hate Catholicism
to see it as a dangerous ideology – a threat –
and I believed that fervently – until
at twenty, I set out into the world, in France
I was caught up in jostling crowds – pilgrims,
so many of them, as if the entire human race was
some boundless river, coursing swift to the kingdom of heaven
I was carried by that current to Rome,
and God showed me his Church – the Catholic Church –
and there – oh God, the things I saw
my heart beat harder – I could barely breathe
the pillars, arches, architecture, all lifting

our perception of this world into the sky.
The Protestant faith I'd followed hates the arts
deprives its world of colour – and of light –
and says the naked word should be enough
so I had never felt the power of art – but
now, the music of the heavens fell like spring rain
from the ceilings of the churches, and
I could see – and hear – and touch – pure holiness
in the world – I saw the Pope say mass – and bless / the people,

MARY   Stop. No more.
Your words unfurl a life in front of me
there's *hope,* a whole new path rolls out like silk
but I can't take a step – my feet are chained

MORTIMER   My mind had been in chains. But now – it's *free.*
The Protestant Church had been my cold, bare cell
but now, your majesty, I saw the light
I swore myself a Catholic – and I met
your relative / the Cardinal of Lorraine

MARY   the Cardinal of Lorraine – oh is he well? That man,
that beautiful man is a rock of the Church
he mentored me in France when I was young
and this letter is from him

MORTIMER   Yes – he spoke to me,
in his hands I confirmed my Catholic faith
and he, my holy teacher, sent me then
to Rheims, where I met your followers, Morgan,
and the Bishop of Ross, and in his home
My eyes were opened: windows to the soul
and God's wide world is there for us to *see* –
I saw your face – a picture – seeing you
my soul was shaken.

,

'The most beautiful woman', the Bishop said quietly,
'is also the most desperate, the martyr
of our faith.' My eyes filled up with tears.

27

'And it is England where she is in prison,
surrounded by our enemies, alone.'

MARY   There's hope – there's hope while that man is alive

MORTIMER I didn't take his word for it – the books I read
the scholars that I spoke to – everything
confirms this single fact, this *primal* fact: that
your bloodline and your lineage prove you are
the rightful Queen of England. Not this illegal Queen
of tainted blood – born from adultery
a bastard called a bastard by the King
her own royal father cut her off at birth
tore down Elizabeth's claim to take his crown
The wrong you suffer is because they know
you are the rightful heir of England's throne.
The kingdom you should rule imprisons you.

MARY   That right has been the cause of endless wrong –

MORTIMER And then news came the prisoner was transferred
they'd moved you – and my uncle was your jailer!
The hand of God had opened up a door
to help us get to you – we made a plan
The Cardinal and all our friends agreed
move fast: ten days ago, I landed here.

,

And then I saw you.

No light or beauty in these rooms you live in
but still – your light – holy, angelic light –
shines out. I think Elizabeth is wise
to keep you hidden – if your face was seen,
rebellion – if the people saw their Queen
a wave of blood would roll across the land
a violent revolution. But we don't have long
it's dangerous: and I must tell you the news –

MARY   Have I been sentenced? Tell me – I can take it –

MORTIMER   Your sentence has been passed. The forty-two
           high judges reached their verdict: *guilty.*

           ,

           The Queen's advisers, and the House of Lords
           the House of Commons and the City of London
           all scream that sentence must be carried out –
           but the Queen still delays. Not for human reasons
           [but] political ones: it's tactics, not conscience:
           she knows they'll force her hand, eventually.

           MARY speaks with composure, but fear rises in her now like water.

MARY   I'm not surprised. I knew that this was coming.
           I know there's no way now they'll set me free –
           and so they'll keep me prisoner here forever –
           that way my claim dies with me / in my cell

MORTIMER   No – no – your majesty, they won't stop at prison.
           While you're alive, so is Elizabeth's fear –
           her only route to safety is your death –

MARY   You think the Queen would execute a queen?

MORTIMER   I do: she would. She will, make no mistake.

MARY   But France would declare war to get revenge –

MORTIMER   The rumour is she's going to give her hand
           in marriage to the heir to France's throne

MARY   The day she has my head down on the block
           she doubles every danger to her own:
           her power rolls with my head in the dust
           what would the word 'queen' mean after my death?

MORTIMER   Elizabeth's own mother, Anne Boleyn
           and Katherine Howard – and Lady Jane Grey
           were queens – of England – and they lost their heads

           ,

29

MARY   You're scared, I know. This terror's hard to think through.
                But it's not just the scaffold I'm afraid of:
                Elizabeth has subtler options open
                to wipe away my challenge to her throne
                A public execution is a risk
                but paying someone silently to do it?
                I cannot take a sip of water here
                without the thought that –

MORTIMER   Listen – don't be scared
                our plan is underway, it's happening now:
                just this morning – twelve young men – I'm one –
                have sworn to get you out of here by force.

                MARY really is afraid of that, angry –

MARY   What are you *thinking*? Don't you understand?
                Have you not seen the heads nailed up on bridges
                my friends' dead flesh pulled open as a warning
                to anyone who tries to fight for me?
                Just *GO – get out of here* – god knows that Burleigh
                already somehow will be on your trail –
                the friends of Mary Stuart end up dead.

MORTIMER   Yes, I have seen the heads nailed up on bridges
                and dead men's flesh pulled open as a warning
                and no, in no way do they frighten me
                because they died and won eternal glory
                and death for what is right is *martyrdom*

MARY   Keep your voice down. As clever as you are,
                whatever force you use: *I can't be saved.*
                They're watching everywhere and everything
                it's not just Paulet, or the swarms of spies,
                it's all of England guards these prison gates.
                Elizabeth alone could open them

MORTIMER   There is no chance

MARY   There is one man who could

MORTIMER   Name him.

MARY   The Earl of Leicester.

MORTIMER   Leicester?
The Earl of Leicester, the favourite of the Queen?
The man who argues daily for your death?
I / hardly think

MARY   If anyone can save me, it's him.
Go to him. Speak to him: [include] everything. And –

KENNEDY runs in.

MARY suddenly produces a letter from her person –

and give him this. I've carried it for weeks –
in hope that somehow it could get to Leicester

MORTIMER Explain

MARY   Someone's coming – please: trust Leicester
And he will trust you – he'll explain the mystery

KENNEDY It's Paulet with another man – from court

MORTIMER That's Burleigh. Act surprised, your majesty.

MORTIMER exits.

*PAULET and BURLEIGH enter. BURLEIGH is official, exacting,
unforgiving.*

*This rush of possibility seems to have done something to MARY – she's
brave.*

PAULET   You asked me earlier for certainty:
Lord Burleigh brings it. Listen patiently.

MARY   – with all the dignity of innocence.

BURLEIGH I speak now with the voice of England's law.

MARY   You constantly rewrite it – so it's right
it sounds like you.

BURLEIGH   It seems to me you know your sentence.

MARY   Your presence here, Lord Burleigh, makes it clear.
              Please carry on.

BURLEIGH   Lady Mary Stuart, you willingly
              were subject to the court / of forty-two –

MARY   Lord Burleigh, I'm so sorry to interrupt
              right at the start – just as you're setting off –
              you say that I 'was subject to the court'.
              A queen is not a subject – cannot be
              a subject, unless I give away my right,
              my royal prerogative – my rank
              the honour of my people – and my son
              (and actu'ally, the whole notion of the monarch)
              At the foundation of the English law
              is this precept: that any citizen
              accused of crimes, is afforded the right
              to trial before a jury of his peers.
              Who is my peer among those forty-two?
              Kings are my only peers.

BURLEIGH   You heard the charges

MARY   I heard the charges so I could reply
              and demonstrate that I was innocent.

BURLEIGH   and you submitted to the questions of the court.

MARY   I answered questions only to respect
              the noble lords – themselves – but *not* the court
              which I reject.

BURLEIGH   Whether you reject the court or not,
              it's just irrelevant formality:
              you're breathing England's air. Its laws *apply*.

MARY   I breathe the air inside an English prison.
              In what way do those laws help me in here?
              I'm not from England – I don't know your laws
              I'm not a citizen of this country
              I'm queen of a completely different state

BURLEIGH   And so you think that the mere name of 'Queen'
             entitles you – in countries you don't rule –
             to stir up treasonous rebellion?

MARY   Of course I am accountable to justice
             It's just your *judges* are not fit to judge

BURLEIGH is rattled now.

BURLEIGH   *Our judges* – in your eyes, apparently,
             are nobodies we've picked up off the streets
             just mouthpieces, we've bribed them, probably,
             they're just the tools of England's brute oppression.
             In fact, they've served us selflessly *for years*
             they are the *best men of this government*
             and what would *you* have done, 'Your Majesty',
             if *you* were Queen of England in this case?
             What better strategy could you recommend
             pray tell, than this: appoint the noblest men
             the *fairest* you could find, the best respected,
             and let those men serve justice in this case?
             Let's even say we hated you so much
             that some of them *were* bribed to vote against you
             (they weren't) – still: forty-two of them? Hard to control
             forty two – quite a large number to *corrupt*
             and looking at the verdict, that seems clear
             when *forty-one votes* sentence you to death.

             ,

MARY   I'm surprised. I'm an uneducated woman
             how can I match a speaker of such skill?
             You're right. Before the judges you describe
             I'd have no choice but to accept their sentence:
             their honour would make their judgement sacrosanct.
             But, problem is, in recent history,
             these men have not been pillars of the law
             it seems to me that they've been more like whores
             attending to the whims of my great-uncle
             Henry the Eighth (a man who loved his flatterers)
             it seems to me that, under him, the Lords

and your beloved House of Commons – would
enact a law, and then repeal that law
dissolve a marriage, now enforce that marriage
especially if *that marriage* is the key
to changing bastard daughters into queens
(I only call them bastards as they were
declared as such *in law* by – yes – those men)
and changing daughters into queens is not
the only changing they've been getting on with:
the *state religion* flip-flopped *four times over*
four religions under *four regimes*

BURLEIGH You said before you don't know England's laws
you seem to know our miseries all right

MARY Be fair with me – and I'll be fair with you.
They say you're honest, loyal, unbribable
They say you're driven by more than your own gain
We'll go with that. So. Please. You can't mistake
true justice for the politics of the state.
What is the logic of a 'trial by equals'?
It's this: we only trust people like us.
How can you judge someone who isn't you?
How could a Scotsman judge an Englishman
when they're *unlike*, in history and in culture?
Or zealous Catholic judge a Protestant?
Or commoner a queen – or man a woman?
There is deep custom in these differences
they hold their separate wisdoms, and we should
respect them – but there is a time for unity
and empathy. Do you not ever think
our countries are one island on the world
one circled space of ground for us to walk
one chalky rock, beaten about by green seas
and yes, two separate lands, but then, my Lord
those borders we created – in our minds –
imaginary lines – that cut the land in half
there's nothing in our geography to split
the top half from the bottom – yet, for years,
for centuries, we've only been at war

we tear things up when we could come together
nor will that (needless) conflict ever cease
until these lands are *one* –

BURLEIGH   and [presumably] ruled by *you*?

MARY   Oh, why deny it now?
It's true that once I thought I might bring peace
and unity to these two lands – at last.

BURLEIGH   You set out to achieve that with *division*:
by kindling civil war to get the throne

MARY   *(Ferocious.)* I did not – *did not* do that! Show me PROOF

BURLEIGH   I didn't come to argue. Anyway
the time for making arguments is past.

By forty-one votes out of forty-two
the court decrees that Lady Mary Stuart
deliberately violated last year's Act
of Parliament, and thus incurs the sentence –
'If any person makes Rebellion
against the Queen, or claims Title to her Crown,
they shall be prosecuted / by the law
and / if found guilty, shall be put to death'

MARY   Sir – sir – Lord Burleigh.
It's pretty likely I'll be guilty of a law
conceived and passed expressly to convict me:
the same few men, your judges, *wrote* that Act!
And even *you* can't – please – try to deny
that this Act was a trap designed for me –

BURLEIGH   It was a warning. *You* made it a trap
when you conspired to kill the Queen of England
with Babington and his accomplices
the actors of a plot that you devised

MARY   And how could I have done that?

BURLEIGH   Well, you did –
and from your cell you masterminded treason

MARY   So where's the evidence – the *proof* of that?

BURLEIGH   You saw the documents yourself in court

MARY   *(With irony.)* The *letters* that are so unlike my writing
                you had to claim that I dictated them

BURLEIGH   No, *Babington* said that you'd dictated them
                and sent them to him. Swore it, under oath,
                Then he was put to death. But on the record
                he testified the letters came from you

MARY   But he was not a witness at my trial.
                It would surely have been better to hear
                key evidence in person? No? Lord Burleigh,
                why *was* there such a rush to have him dead?

BURLEIGH   Your secretaries verified his story.
                They said they'd written down the words you spoke.

MARY   So now my *servants* are my judges too!

BURLEIGH   You said your Scottish staff could all be trusted

MARY   Yes – but history is written *at the end*
                after the fact. So what they *actually said*
                compared to what the court recorded – well
                [if] you torture people, they'll confess to things
                sometimes to things they'd never even *thought of.*
                Perhaps they knew it couldn't get much worse
                for *me*, and lied so *they* could stay alive

BURLEIGH   They gave their testimony under oath

MARY   But not in court. Hang on – they're still alive –
                why not just call my secretaries here
                and let them speak their evidence to my face?

BURLEIGH   I think that is –

MARY   – *that is* my legal right.
                My former keeper, Talbot, said himself
                the English law is clear on this: the defendant
                in any trial *must* hear the accusation,

36

the criminal hears the evidence against him.
Your predecessor said that, Paulet. No?
Is that not right? You value honesty, I think –
employ it now. That is the law? Yes? Speak!

PAULET   That is the law. I'm sorry – but it is!

MARY   So
The law's enforced whenever it does me harm
Ignored if it might prove my innocence.
So at my makeshift trial, where *was that* law?
And why was Babington not kept alive
until his evidence could be admitted?
And why not call my secretaries in?
they're still alive – why not bring them to court?

BURLEIGH   This is a waste of time. Your plot with Babington
is not the only charge that stands against you

MARY   It is the only charge that breaks that law
the law you all designed to take my life

BURLEIGH   You negotiated with the ambassador of Spain –

MARY   And now we change the subject!

BURLEIGH   – you made plans
to overthrow the religion of this state,
you instigated all the kings of Europe
to wage a war on England

MARY   If I did?
Would anyone be shocked or horrified?
I'm innocent of every charge against me –
but were I guilty, would you be surprised?
I came to England as a refugee
seeking asylum, I came here for *help*
to beg for mercy from my blood relation
Elizabeth – who, instead, had me *locked up*
which violates all international laws
and constitutes an act of warfare.
I don't believe – now look, sir, do you think

37

and let's be honest – do you *really* think
that I owe any moral debt to England?
Or that the English law is fair? Or just?
How can I possibly accept these chains
around my neck – having done nothing wrong? –
There's just so many questions – like how you
can justify detaining me in law?
and how are other nations, hearing this,
not forced to turn to force to match the force
with which Elizabeth holds me in here?
This is *war*. And in a war, some violence is just,
and reasonable – but even so – my conscience
would *never* sanction regicide.
Lord Burleigh, I could never kill Elizabeth:
the stain of murder would dishonour me –
dishonour – not 'make me subject to your laws'.
But regardless of your laws, this is not justice
this is a power struggle – this is force.

BURLEIGH   Well, if it is: then she is on the throne
and you are not. You're powerless. You're here.

MARY hands the sentencing document back to BURLEIGH.

MARY   So she is strong and I am weak –
So be it. Let your tyrant queen use force
and slaughter me to make her crown secure
A queen's head coming off like anyone's
is not a precedent I'd be keen to set
but if she murders me, the world will *know*
she used brute force 'cause she was scared of justice
and everything she hides behind her mask
will be exposed – and it won't look too good,
won't look like holiness or virginity or the law
but just like *tyranny* – which is what it *IS*.

MARY exits.

BURLEIGH   She'll be defiant till her head is off.
She knew that sentence, somehow. Not a tear

she didn't even blink. And she knows the Queen
is wavering – and our panic makes her brave

PAULET   She's right, though, on Babington and the secretaries
That trial cut corners. They should have been in court.

BURLEIGH *(Fast.)* Too risky. Look – just now – the way she speaks
her power over people's minds is clear –
and when she *cries* – She'd get them to retract.

PAULET   But now there's rumours everywhere that we
corrupted English law for our own ends.

BURLEIGH And that's the thing that persecutes the Queen.
Whichever way she moves, things fall apart –
and Mary Stuart's really several things:
she's Catholic, she's the heir (or so she thinks)
and she's a female monarch.

          ,

          I wish she'd died before she got to England.

PAULET   It would have saved us all a lot of trouble.

BURLEIGH Or if she'd caught something – and died in prison.
Though then no doubt they'd still say it was murder.

PAULET   Well, you can't stop people thinking

BURLEIGH   Still,
there'd be no proof. And likely, fewer rumours.

PAULET   I wouldn't dwell on rumours.

BURLEIGH   The thing is, Paulet,
the rumours come regardless of the facts
attacking genuine justice just as much
as – things we've done that we'd prefer to hide.
The English public love an underdog,
they always hate the person who's on top.
And they prefer their justice from a man.
so in this case, it's practically *unseemly*
for a woman to kill a woman. Yes – I know –

39

but if the Queen were male? A different story.
The forty-two of us wasted our time –
the trial, the sentencing – a waste of time:
the consequences fall on the Queen's head.
if Mary dies, then God knows what comes next,
but it won't go unnoticed by the world.
The fact that she's alive in here's a *risk*
but execution could be even worse.
The Queen still has the right to grant her pardon –
and that's what she should do –

PAULET   And let her live?

BURLEIGH   No – she cannot stay alive – she cannot live
[Be]cause every day she does, the danger grows:
alive, she breeds rebellion from this cell
but if she's killed, then untold retribution
the fear – the *fact* – her people will strike back
and that's the cage this case has locked the Queen in,
where every move available is wrong.
And sometimes you can see she wants to act –
but – no – the words can't pass her lips.
She's waiting for someone to take the hint.
Hoping someone saves her from this choice
of 'merciful but weak' or 'brutal tyrant'

PAULET   Well, that's the choice. It isn't going to change.

BURLEIGH   I think the Queen thinks that it could. If she
just had some more attentive servants –

PAULET   attentive?

BURLEIGH   Someone to hear her *un*spoken commands.

                ,

PAULET   I'll just remind you – what my duty is –
I guard whoever I've been asked to guard

BURLEIGH   But if we'd said 'protect this poisonous snake'?
An enemy is different from a jewel

PAULET   A reputation is a jewel. I mean
                the Queen's good name must also be protected

BURLEIGH   Look, Paulet, when we moved the prisoner here –

PAULET   – you chose the most dependable pair of hands
                to keep this critical situation safe.
                If not, Lord Burleigh, then you got it wrong.

                ,

BURLEIGH   The news gets out: the Stuart queen is ill
                she worsens, week by week – and then she dies.
                That way, the people gradually forget her
                and you keep your hands clean

PAULET   But not my conscience

BURLEIGH   *(Angry.)* If you're refusing to co-operate
                I trust you won't object to someone / else [killing her] –

PAULET   *For God's sake* I will fight the man myself
                if someone tries to harm her in this prison
                No murderer will get beyond this door
                as long as my name's on the bloody warrant.
                Her life is in my hands – and honestly
                Elizabeth's life is no more sacred here
                than Mary's is. She's here under my guard.
                You bring me a signed warrant for her death,
                I'll happily let your men take her away.
                But until there's public process, under law
                she stays here and her hands stay tied, of course
                but she will stay alive. Keep your business above board.

ACT TWO

The palace of Westminster.

DAVISON   Excuse me, is it Kent? You're back sooner than we thought
Have the festivities all been and gone?

KENT   Were you not there? Did you not watch the games?

DAVISON   My duties held me here.

KENT   You missed quite the sight.
They put a play on – an expensive one:
The Virgin Fortress (it's a metaphor)
under siege from the troops of *Desire.* There were songs.
Desire's troops were French, of course, you know
the way these foreign visits work – but still
the cannons fired rich perfumes through the air
and silken petals rained down onto us
but, in the end, the troops were beaten back:
Desire had to retreat; the castle stood.

DAVISON   That's not an omen of good news to come
for this French marriage suit. Who set that up?

KENT   No, no, it was a joke – tell you the truth,
I think our Castle's planning to surrender –

DAVISON   I can't believe she'll actually give in –

KENT   The articles that were the sticking points
have been agreed – and France has given in.
The Prince can have his Catholic services
in secret, and behind closed doors at home
in public, though, he toes the party line
a practising, committed Protestant
who honours the religion of the state.
Don't look like that: the public mood is tense
and panicked – and their will is crystal clear: in fact
she knows a royal wedding's what they want

they know at some point she is going to die
and Virgin Queens cannot produce an heir
she dies without an heir – and chaos reigns
and (this is why the public's terrified)
Queen Mary Stuart claims the English throne
and England becomes Catholic again.

DAVISON   But Mary Stuart is an empty fear:
the day Elizabeth weds the Prince of France
the same day, Mary's head goes on the block

KENT   She's older than you think.

Enter QUEEN ELIZABETH I, with AUBESPINE, the French ambassador. The Earl of LEICESTER, Lord BURLEIGH, and Lord TALBOT assemble.

ELIZABETH   I'm sorry, sir, that you were sent to England
I'm sure you must miss France – the ladies there
are younger – lovelier – than here in England
at least, more lovely than we are ourselves
and yes, your views are better –

AUBESPINE   Well, though your country has but one royal lady
it's lucky she is the pinnacle of her sex
and quite delightful.

ELIZABETH   Flattering – *(She's forgotten his name.)*

BURLEIGH   – Lord Aubespine

AUBESPINE   Your majesty, I beg your leave to go
and take the joyful news back to the Prince
(His heart is so impatient that he couldn't
wait for us to get to Paris – so
he's in Amiens, waiting for the news)

ELIZABETH   Don't ask us to repeat ourselves, Lord Aubespine
We've said we cannot wear a wedding dress
when England's sky is ominous and black:
the threats against us rain down thick and fast
against us, and our courtiers – and my life

43

AUBESPINE Then just give us your *promise*, Your Majesty
the happy day can wait for happier days.

Something gives in ELIZABETH. It could be a swing in honesty's
direction rather than anger's, but everyone except AUBESPINE is used
to the queen's volatility, and readies themselves.

ELIZABETH A king is just a slave to being king.
The condition of a monarch is captivity,
hard labour: we may not follow our heart.
If it were my choice, I would live unmarried
and for my epitaph all I want is this:
'Here lies the Virgin Queen'.
My subjects, though, do not want that at all
and cast their minds *beyond* my funeral:
it's not enough that England prospers *now*
when there's a *future* I could help provide for.
I've given them my mind, my warlike arm
a whole lifetime of service – not enough
my virginity is now the thing they want
they'll take that too – and force me down the aisle.
I really thought I'd ruled them like a man
but what they're saying is 'No, you're just a woman.'
No, it's not enough to be a queen
relentlessly undaunted by the task
it's not enough to make the right decisions
time after time after time – it's not enough
that I don't dream the day away – but get things done –
you'd think that might exempt me from the law
the blind and meaningless – but natural – law
that takes one half of the entire human race
and beats it down, subservient to the other

,

AUBESPINE You've been – you are – an exemplary queen.
And there's no man alive worthy enough
that you should sacrifice your freedom for him.
But – if there were, for handsomeness, and birth
and virtue / not accounting for

44

ELIZABETH   A marriage with France would have advantages,
I'm quite aware of that, Ambassador.
Let me be honest – if that's what has to happen
if public pressure forces me to yield
(and their will is much stronger than my own)
then there's no Prince in Europe that I would
less reluctantly surrender to than France.
Those words are all I have for you for now
I'm sure you'll find some hope in there somewhere

AUBESPINE It is a wonderful hope – but it's just a hope –
the Prince of France wants something more

ELIZABETH   Like *what*?

                        ,

*ELIZABETH might be about to lose her temper – but then changes
her mind somehow. She takes off a ring from her finger. Looks at it.
Tension mounts: is this going to be the wedding?*

A little ring. A little circled gold.
This ring means different things in different places.
It's duty – but it's also slavery:
two rings can start a marriage – or a chain.
You may take this – and give it to His Highness
it's – well – non-binding. It's not yet a chain
but it could grow – and bind me to a king.

He kneels and accepts the ring.

AUBESPINE In his name, I accept your gift, Great Queen.
I kiss your hand to signify his thanks.
Your mercy is an honour to behold.
This is a day of joy. May God extend
that joy to everyone in England –
perhaps including that unhappy Queen
whose fate concerns France and England alike / and

ELIZABETH *Enough of that.* Ambassador, let's not mix
two things that aren't compatible.
Our future husband must share our concerns.
and not be friendly with our enemy.

45

AUBESPINE   Your Majesty, forgive me, but you would
doubt the nobility of France if we
forgot the widow of our King – and fellow
believer, in our Faith. Humanity
and honour both demand –

ELIZABETH   I take that point
above the line, as surely you intend.
France may well choose to play the friend
but I will act as queen.

She nods her head once. AUBESPINE bows and leaves.

ELIZABETH sits down. The Council is in session.

BURLEIGH   Your Highness, you have crowned your people's wishes.
The future is assured. We can enjoy
with confidence the peace you've given us.
One thing alone remains. There is just one
one last request your country begs you grant.

ELIZABETH   And what more do my people want?

BURLEIGH   Her head.
The Stuart's head would set your people free.
They want assurance that her threat to you
is cauterised. There's rumours everywhere
that Catholic cells are *here in our own country*
cherishing their faith in secret – and – wait
they want a war against the English throne
and your annihilation is its aim
there's Catholic networks operating *now*
assassins sent out secretly from Rheims
and landing on our shores – and this we know
three times already we've intercepted them
we've caught the traitors hiding in our court
but why continue that? In Fotheringay
we've *got* the goddess of their holy war
the flame that gives them their fanatic hope
and holds our national safety over the fire –
there is no peace with them: their aims are clear:
to break the Stuart from her prison cell

and set her firmly down upon your throne.
My lady, it is cut and dried – it's this:
if we won't pull the trigger, we get shot.
Her life is death to you – your death, her life.

ELIZABETH I know, Lord Burleigh, that your passion comes
from loyalty and wisdom. All the same
I hate it from the bottom of my soul.
I don't like wisdom when it's smeared in blood.
I want more moderate options –

*TALBOT speaks from the heart – battered with time. He's older, somehow
more direct, more sincere than his colleagues on the council.*

TALBOT   In my heart
I feel the zeal Lord Burleigh feels, your Majesty,
and this Council must ensure that England's safe
and keep you on your throne for years to come
and keep our future bright. But security
sits side by side with reputation –
your glorious name, the respect that you command.
We must be careful to protect that too

ELIZABETH Of course we must, my lord. What are you saying?

TALBOT That there are other roads open to you
than beheading Mary Stuart. That her sentence
whether we like it or not – is illegal.
You cannot be her judge – or pass her sentence
when she is not your subject

ELIZABETH   In that case
this Council and my Parliament and the Law
have got it wrong. They say I *can* do that.

TALBOT A majority does not prove a thing is right.
England is not the world. Your Parliament
does not comprise the entire human race.
England today and England yesterday
are different things – and different from tomorrow's [England]
Things change – and world opinion changes too
it rises and it falls with England's tides

ELIZABETH   The opinion of my *people* does not change.

TALBOT   You say your people are your master here
They're not. Let's test that. Exercise free will.
Just say – you say – you don't want to shed blood
say that in public – say you are for *peace*
say that you *want* to save Queen Mary's life,
shut down the people who would speak against it,
and this deadlock will vanish – they'll accept: *you chose.*
But *you* must make this judgement. You alone.
Your *own* command is what you must obey
advice like ours is insecure – at best

ELIZABETH   You put my enemy's case quite beautifully
I must say I would rather hear *my own*

TALBOT   Her case has not been made by anyone!
We've blocked her from her lawful right
of legal council – and there's no man else
will stick his neck out [by] putting Mary's side.
I'm old, I'm close to death, so I don't spin
my words to try and climb the ladder:
but let it not be said, Your Majesty,
that in your royal council, selfishness
and pure self-interest hoarded all the votes
made all the noise – while *mercy* just sat silent.
The whole of England stands against that woman
You've never seen her with your own two eyes
And why would anyone pity a total stranger?
Now I'm not saying she's a saint – she's not
But she's just a woman locked in prison. Weak

ELIZABETH   Women are not weak. Some of us are strong.
I will not have you say that in my presence

TALBOT   You're strong because your life was hard. No throne
was promised you at birth, no flatterers
told you each day how wonderful you were,
you were locked in the Tower, you had your faith
and that was all. But God did not save Mary.
Raised a Catholic, raised in France and called

a queen when she could barely sign her name,
and brainwashed with it all – she never heard
the voice of truth: it was drowned out
in giddy whirling golden false frivolities
and she was the most beautiful young girl
and having royal blood [it's not surprising –]

ELIZABETH   Let me remind you that
this is a formal meeting of the council,
Lord Talbot. That might have slipped your mind
though I must say, her beauty must be something
to inspire such excitement in a pensioner.

,

The Earl of Leicester is extremely quiet.
Does Mary Stuart not fire up your tongue?

LEICESTER   I'm silent in astonishment, your Majesty,
to think that rumours from the common street
well, fairy tales, that scare the gullible
have risen to the level of this council.
I'm really quite surprised, I have to say
that Mary, Queen of Scots (though not a queen
in fact – she couldn't hold her tiny throne)
that Mary former Queen of Scots, an exile
an exile running scared from her own country
can suddenly breed such terror in a queen.
For God's sake – why are you so scared of her?
Because she claims your throne? Or do we think
a peaceful, Protestant England will – on a whim –
renounce its faith and turn back to the Pope?
There's nothing in me that can understand
this anguish on the question of succession
this push to get you married – I don't know
quite honestly why your councillors seem so panicked.
You're young. She's old. For years to come, you'll dance
over her grave: [there's] no need to push her in.

BURLEIGH   It seems the Earl of Leicester's changed his mind

49

LEICESTER   I voted for her death sentence *in court*
but in this private Council, my advice
is *practical* – the best thing for the Queen
Your Majesty, it seems a senseless time
to murder her, when France has left her side
and come to *yours, and* you look to *marry* France
(renewing hope that you'll produce an heir)
and she's in prison. She's *already dead.*
being hated by the public *is* a death
your mercy would just bring her back to life.

BURLEIGH   Is there a recommendation here, Lord Leicester?

LEICESTER   There is, my lord. We let her sentence stand
and let her live, but living underneath
a sharpened blade, held inches from her neck
the second *any* uprising begins –
it falls.

,

ELIZABETH   My lords, I've heard your thoughts – and thank you for
your passionate advice concerning this.
With God's assistance, I will think it through
and come to a decision.

Enter PAULET, bringing with him MORTIMER.

                   Lord Paulet
What have you got for us?

PAULET   My nephew, Mortimer.
He has returned, your Majesty, from France
from Rheims – and kneels now at your feet.
I recommend him to your royal favour.

MORTIMER   Long live Your Majesty. God save the Queen.

MORTIMER kneels, ELIZABETH beckons him up.

ELIZABETH   Well, welcome back to England, Mortimer.
You've been on quite the Catholic tour. So tell us
how our enemies are getting on?

MORTIMER   I met the Scottish exiles who, at Rheims
           are plotting violence against your throne:
           I won their trust

PAULET   They gave him coded letters
           to give to Mary: he brought them to *us*.

ELIZABETH   What are our enemies planning?

MORTIMER   They were shocked
           when France abandoned them to come to you.
           They're looking now to Spain.

ELIZABETH   Yes, so we hear.

MORTIMER   There is another thing

ELIZABETH   We are all ears

MORTIMER   The Pope has excommunicated you.
           The Papal bill had just arrived from Rome
           that sealed in law your banishment from their Faith
           you're now an enemy of the Catholic Church.

LEICESTER   Such weapons don't hurt England any more

BURLEIGH   They could if they were in fanatic hands

        ELIZABETH is looking at MORTIMER.

ELIZABETH   I've heard that you renounced our faith in Rheims.

           ,

MORTIMER   That was only my disguise, your majesty
           deliberately – to better serve *your* cause

        *PAULET has chosen this moment to put a letter into ELIZABETH's
        hands.*

ELIZABETH   What is it?

PAULET   It's a letter from the Queen
           of Scots

BURLEIGH   Give that to me

PAULET   You have no *right!*
        She charged me to deliver it to the Queen
        and not to you. A criminal still has rights.

ELIZABETH looks at both of them. Then, opens the letter. As she
reads it, MORTIMER and LEICESTER secretly exchange a few words.
BURLEIGH is not happy with PAULET.

BURLEIGH   What does it say, then?

PAULET   She made no secret of it
        She asks the Queen to meet her face to face.

BURLEIGH   *(Fast.)* Well that must never be allowed to happen!

TALBOT   Why not? What *possibly* could be the problem there?

BURLEIGH   You plot to kill the Lord's Anointed Queen [then]
        you lose the right to put your case to her!

TALBOT   So if your Queen *desires* to show her mercy
        then you're opposed to that?

BURLEIGH   She's *had her sentence!*
        She's going to lose her head – so what is gained
        by letting her Majesty see the corpse-to-be?
        If those two meet, then mercy is *implied*
        it makes a mockery of the court, the law –

ELIZABETH makes a noise. The letter has moved her to tears.

,

She dries her eyes.

ELIZABETH   Oh what *are* humans? What *happens* on earth?
        our happiness, our fragile, fragile lives?
        Nothing.
        You read this – and you think, she *was* a queen
        born to the oldest throne in Christendom
        who once had hopes to be the Queen of England
        and of Scotland and of France. This letter here –
        so different from the way she used to write,
        so changed. It's sad. And it hurts me to think

the ground beneath our feet is so unfirm,
that we might fall. How easily it comes.

TALBOT God speaks to you, Your Majesty, and puts
his mercy in your heart – listen to it!
She's guilty, she's been punished for her crime
and now this thing must end. Put out your hand
to her – let her *speak* to you

BURLEIGH   Your Majesty
be steadfast. Don't let emotion cloud your mind,
admirable sentiment though it is.
You have to do the thing that must be done:
She's sentenced – can't be pardoned, can't be saved
and if you meet her, none of that will change
and so it just looks cruel – you went to gloat
before she lost her head

LEICESTER   I think we might
remember where the boundaries are, my lords.
The Queen is wise, and she does not require
assistance in deciding what to do.
A private conference between the queens
would be quite separate from the course of law.
The *law* has passed its sentence, *not* the *crown.*
The Queen can do whatever her heart desires
and not affect the course of law at all.

ELIZABETH My lords, you are dismissed. We will find ways
to bring the two together – necessity
and mercy – and make them one.

Everyone leaves. At the door, she calls, noticed by PAULET –

                                        Mortimer –

*She looks at him again. There's something sexual in this look, though
ELIZABETH hasn't yet decided whether she trusts MORTIMER. So
ELIZABETH and MORTIMER are dangerous to each other – and that's
erotic. He steps back towards her.*

It's brave to live inside your enemy's camp
it takes great self control – a special thing
in a young man. It suggests a golden future.
And we can make that prophecy come true.

MORTIMER My hand is yours, Your Majesty, my life
is dedicated to your service.

ELIZABETH   Well
You met my enemies – and England's, too
their hate for me is inexhaustible
and now they come to kill me. Thank the Lord
so far we have been saved – but for how long?
While she's alive, my crown shakes on my head.

MORTIMER She dies whenever you give the command

ELIZABETH A-ha! I thought we'd moved in that direction
but actually we've stood completely still.
Our thought was – let the legal system work
and then her blood comes nowhere near our hands.
The law has passed its sentence. Here we are.
What happens now? It must be *executed*.
And who must order execution? Me.
The bloody deed lands right back in my lap
but now – and worse – does so in public view

MORTIMER Why do you care about how things appear?
You have just cause.

ELIZABETH   And you don't know the world.
The way that things appear is *what they are*
and people don't look deeper, don't dig down
into the complex, double-sided truth of things.
One glance – that's final judgement. As for me,
my people seem to want the Stuart dead
but there's no way that they'll think I'm in the right
when my signature's on the warrant for her head
and so we work to cloak her death in doubt
at least, my part in it. The deed has double form.
Confess a step one way – you pay the price

and so the only safety is to cloud
the water, mask the steps you take.

MORTIMER It would be for the best then if [someone else killed her] –

ELIZABETH *(Fast.)* Exactly.
My best angel speaks through you. Continue, please
complete your thought. You're different from your uncle.

MORTIMER Has he been asked?

ELIZABETH He has

MORTIMER He's very strict.

,

ELIZABETH Are *you* reliable?

MORTIMER I said, my hand is yours.
And you can save your reputation.

ELIZABETH Yes
And perhaps one morning you can wake me up
to tell me 'Mary Stuart died last night'.

MORTIMER I think I can

ELIZABETH How long – how long before
my sleep improves?

MORTIMER Before the next new moon.

ELIZABETH Well. Farewell, sir.
I know you'll understand if gratitude
is forced to come in secret – and by night.
Silence is the god of happy men.
The closest bonds – the tenderest –
are those that are not seen.

ELIZABETH leaves.

Whose side is MORTIMER on?

MORTIMER Duplicitous, bloody, hypocrite woman!
As you lie to the world, I lie to you
dishonesty is purity in your court.
And every hour you wait for me to kill her
her rescue mission gathers speed – and force.
And what reward do you think you can offer?
Your body? I'd only touch it with a *knife*
There is a queen whose soul radiates *life*
she is the way to heaven – you're just earth.
You haven't been in love. You can't feel love.
You think that somehow you can see the truth
inside my eyes, but – no – that's your reflection
Elizabeth: you only see yourself.
You think I'll be your murderer? – I will
but in a second way: I'll murder you.

Enter PAULET.

PAULET What did the Queen say to you?

MORTIMER   Nothing, sir.
Nothing – of importance.

PAULET looks at MORTIMER, honestly – fixed gaze.

PAULET A shiny path you've started walking on
but slippery. You're young. And she's the Queen.
I understand – keep your ambition checked.

MORTIMER You were the one who brought me to her court?

PAULET I wish I hadn't, now. I'm only saying
your conscience is your ruler above all.
Hold fast to that. Don't pay too high a price.

MORTIMER What are you scared of?

PAULET   That you'll trust her word.
She makes big promises – you take commands
you do your half of it – but she's the Queen
she saves her reputation, turns on you
and claims her vengeance for your bloody deed.

MORTIMER I'm sorry, 'bloody deed' –

PAULET   STOP THE PRETENCE
          I *know* the thing the Queen's asked you to do
          You're young, she hopes that you're more pliable
          than your unbending uncle. Did you say yes?

MORTIMER   Uncle

PAULET   If you said yes to her, you're dead to me.

          Enter LEICESTER.

LEICESTER Excuse me, sir. A word with your nephew.
           The Queen is most impressed with him.
           She has transferred the care of Mary Stuart
           from you to him.

           PAULET looks at MORTIMER, and exits. LEICESTER is aware of it.

                              Your uncle seems upset.

MORTIMER I don't know – the unexpected trust
          the Queen has placed in me –

          LEICESTER looks at MORTIMER.

LEICESTER *Can* you be trusted, sir?

MORTIMER   I ask the same of you.

LEICESTER You had something to say to me in secret.

MORTIMER First reassure me that it's not a risk.

LEICESTER And who gives me that guarantee for you?
           Don't be offended, Mortimer, but you exist
           in court as two completely different people.
           And clearly one of them is false. But which?

MORTIMER I see the same in you.

LEICESTER   So – who goes first?

MORTIMER The person with the smaller risk to take
          and / that is you

LEICESTER   that is you. Well. I have influence here
                but one man's word can bring the whole thing down.
                You can speak first. Then I will follow suit.

MORTIMER produces the letter. Necessary to be very careful.

MORTIMER   This letter's from the Queen of Scotland

LEICESTER   What?

LEICESTER reaches for it, looks around, hurriedly opens it. It's obviously very sensitive. His eyes scan the paper: he's adrenalized.

                I'm sure you know already what it says –

MORTIMER   No

LEICESTER   She must have told you

MORTIMER   Not a word
                just said that you'd explain the mystery.
                Though now, your eyes speak volumes

LEICESTER   I know that you have found the Catholic faith.
                Give me your hand. Forgive all the suspicion.
                There's no one in this court that you can trust.
                The times are violent, pressures are extreme
                the only kind of safety is disguise
                that's why I seemed to hate the Queen – Queen Mary
                though honestly the opposite is true –
                Mary and I were almost married once
                long before Darnley, long before all this
                and I had no idea what I was losing
                ambition swept me off, I couldn't see
                her youth or beauty, only that the hand
                I held in mine – her hand – was slight.
                I hoped to win the Queen of England's hand.

MORTIMER   And she loves you, it's said

LEICESTER   Well, so it seemed
                but ten years later, ten lost years of wooing
                of wooing someone so completely *vain*

of being chained to someone else's whims
and toyed with, screamed at, promised things – you're told
that you're the favourite, aren't you lucky?
isn't it great the Queen has chosen you?
but actually your life is hers for years to *play with*
and every day you face a different Queen:
tender – proud – or icy cold – who knows?
but now it's ending, there's a younger model
or actually, there's better politics
you heard, today, the young French prince will play
the leading role I gave ten years to learn
so my descent is coming fast – it's *days*
and as the water pours into my ship
and all my hopes get sodden, I remember
the beauty of Mary's eyes – and Mary's hand – and
then I see the jewel I threw away – that
young ambition is no match for love
that love can wait ten years without a scratch

MORTIMER What are you going to do?

LEICESTER   I'll set her free.

                    ,

          This letter says she has forgiven me
          and that she'll wed me if I rescue her.

MORTIMER Rescue her? You voted for her *death*
          You let her sentence pass without a word
          had I not come to bring her letter here
          a miracle sent by God – you'd never *know*

LEICESTER And you think that it doesn't torture me?
          But I would not have let her die. She won't die now.
          My acting will continue till I can
          find ways – and means – to somehow save her life

MORTIMER They're found. You trusted me: now it's my turn.
          I'm going to set her free. The plan is made
          and everything is ready. They're waiting.

LEICESTER   What?

MORTIMER There's more of us. We break her out with force.

LEICESTER There's more? You're frightening me. Wait. Do they know
           the truth of my allegiance?

MORTIMER   It's all right.
           The plan was made entirely without you
           without you it would still have been achieved
           had she not dragged you in – but you *can* help

LEICESTER Can you assure me absolutely that
           my name has not been mentioned in your plot?

MORTIMER Yes. I'm surprised that you're so cagey
          you said you'd find the way to set her free
          we found it – and we planned it – and you're scared?

LEICESTER This isn't how to do it. Shedding blood
           is dangerous

MORTIMER   Waiting's dangerous too

LEICESTER It's too much of a gamble

MORTIMER   Yes – for you
          because you only want her for your bed – but we
          who want her on her rightful throne
          are far less apprehensive

LEICESTER   With respect
           you're young. You just don't understand the risk.

MORTIMER There isn't time to wait

LEICESTER   The traps are laid
           and you can't see them

MORTIMER   I'm not scared of traps

LEICESTER This needs more thought. You'll ruin everything:
           one night – and years of work are ripped away

MORTIMER Do you think there's time for waiting now?

LEICESTER   If we're discovered, they kill us and her

MORTIMER   Risk nothing and you don't deserve to marry her

LEICESTER   You're not *thinking* or *listening* – this is mad
and stupid and impetuous. You'll kill her.

MORTIMER   And what have you been *thinking* all this time
with all your influence? and you've done *nothing*?
what if I was – as your Queen thinks I am –
a murderer prepared to use the keys
the keys that you came here to hand to me
to walk into her cell, unlock the doors,
and knife her while she sleeps – say I'd do that
just as the Queen expects I will – so please tell me
the steps you'd take, right now, to save her life.

LEICESTER   The Queen gave you that order?

MORTIMER   Yes.

LEICESTER   And you / agreed

MORTIMER   Agreed. While the task is mine, it's no one else's.

LEICESTER   All right. That wins us time.

MORTIMER   We're *losing time*

LEICESTER   Be quiet – let me think – the Queen believes
that you will murder her illicitly
so she can publicly be merciful
Perhaps I can persuade her that she should
as Talbot said, come face to face with her
opponent – Burleigh's probably right that if
she sees Mary's face, she'll see herself
in the same situation – and that thought
will stop her executing Mary's sentence
if empathy can make Elizabeth weak –
well, that's what I should try

MORTIMER   But won't she just
find someone else to carry out the murder?
And even if she doesn't, what will change?

61

Your Queen will *never* free the rightful Queen
she'll let her die in prison – and so then
to set her free, your only means is force
and then you're forced to end where I *begin:*
we break her out of there. Elizabeth
I've heard, has spent the night with you before
so take her to one of your castles, raise an army
imprison *her* – refuse to set her free
until Queen Mary takes her rightful place

LEICESTER smiles.

LEICESTER   And now it's clear that you're entirely mad
you just have no idea how these things work
at least, not here in England. That woman
has every man and everything locked down
and not just in her court. Take my advice
you won't try anything wild or fast or rash

ELIZABETH enters and they hear her.

Get out of here

MORTIMER   So what shall I tell Mary?

LEICESTER   Tell her I love her.

MORTIMER   Tell her that yourself.

MORTIMER exits a split-second before ELIZABETH sees him.

ELIZABETH   And who have you been talking to, my Lord?

LEICESTER is surprised –

LEICESTER   Oh – Mortimer

ELIZABETH   You're startled. What's the matter?

LEICESTER   I've never seen you look so beautiful.
And now – well, what I've lost –

ELIZABETH   What have you lost?

62

LEICESTER   You're playing games with me. I'm losing *you*
                   your heart, your self – we know I'm not a king
                   and so my marriage suit is crumpled up
                   and so your new French husband takes your heart
                   but I defy you – search across the world
                   you'll never find a man whose love for you
                   can equal mine. Your fiancé's never *seen* you
                   so it's political love: he loves your *crown*
                   but I love *you*. You – you – you – you – you – you

ELIZABETH   It's not my fault – it's not even my *choice*
                   for God's sake if I could just ask my heart
                   I'd get a different answer – but I *can't*.
                   Oh why can't I just love the man I love?
                   I'd lift you up – I'd have you wear a crown:
                   I *can't*. But Mary Stuart could – she did –
                   she put the crown just where she wanted it
                   she let her femininity take the rein –
                   followed her appetites – didn't hold back
                   she filled the glass right to the brim – and drank it down

LEICESTER   But it didn't sustain her

ELIZABETH   Nonetheless
                   she didn't care what people thought of her
                   she wore life lightly – easily – with *joy*
                   no chain of duty pulled tight round her neck
                   just ecstasy and pleasure, full and deep
                   I could have been like her – I am *like her*
                   but I chose rigid monarchy – though *she*
                   she won the heart of every single man
                   simply by being a woman – while I
                   I'm male and stern and like a king. She wins.
                   That's men for you: if it smells like sex
                   that's it: they're in, they're sold – and they forget
                   everything that matters. Talbot today
                   disarmed by Mary's charms – and at his age

LEICESTER   He was her jailer – saw her every day
                   Perhaps she got him then

63

ELIZABETH   *Is* she so beautiful?

,

I've heard so much about her face, her eyes
I often think – how much of it is true?
Don't look at me like that

LEICESTER   Sorry – I just –
I have a secret fantasy that I
could – once – in secret – see you next to her:
see you and Mary face to face – and then
see how completely you would *dominate*
and see her see your eyes – and see herself
a cruel reflection – then, of course, you'd know
just as in strategy you've beaten her
as well as virtue, power, politics
in beauty too – in luminosity
the victory is yours.

ELIZABETH She's younger than me

LEICESTER   Well, she doesn't look it
It's suffering. She's old before her time.
If she saw you it would just torture her
her life behind her, you a future bride
and promised to the Prince of France – and she
once had a French husband herself

ELIZABETH That's strange – the similarity. It is torture.

LEICESTER She asked for it – that letter – just say yes
that favour will just feed her agony
by seeing you – your beauty, face to face
a perfect queen – a bride to be – and – *well*
if I were her, I'd rather lose my head:
we watch as what she asked for eats her up.
Your Majesty, your beauty's at its height.
Your radiance is armed to win this war.

ELIZABETH Now would be – no – no – not now, Leicester
I have to think about it – talk to Burleigh

LEICESTER   What Burleigh understands is politics
            the court, the country – and so on – the state
            this isn't that: this is – woman to woman
            you'd do this for the state of your own heart
            and also mine – though on the side, no doubt
            to visit her plays well politically
            it makes you merciful – and makes her weak
            so visit her – and then dispose of her.

ELIZABETH   I hear she's not attended like a queen
            if I see that, then it becomes my fault –
            and she is my relation, after all –
            I shouldn't witness her reduced to that

LEICESTER   You won't – you wouldn't have to see her cell
            or even step inside the prison walls –
            the great hunt is today – let's say you ride
            your royal steed into the castle park
            and we let Mary take a walk outside
            you see her accidentally – total chance
            and if it doesn't suit you, just ride on
            don't say a word

ELIZABETH   If this is a mistake:
            your fault: not mine. I'm doing this for you
            because I know I'm hurting you – and so
            you see our heart – just think what they would *say*
            Leicester commands the Queen – and we obey.

ACT THREE

A park. Perhaps it's sunset. MARY running – fast –

KENNEDY   Come back – it's like you've got *wings* – I can't keep up

MARY   Oh I could drink the air – unfurl my voice
fling it across that huge gold disc, the *sky* –
I am a kid – a child – let out, set free to fly
to soar across the sheer unbroken space
to bound across the meadows – from my grave
I see the earth has crumbled open: I can see the sun
I'm climbing up and out and wide and *free*
I don't know how it's happened – but I'm free

KENNEDY   Your prison walls have just got slightly wider.
You can't see them behind the trees.

MARY   the trees
Oh thank you trees – thank you – you great wise histories
your paper's coarse and shiny, thick, deep, green
leaves block out the painful world – I'm dreaming
I'm held now by the heavens – held up, high
my eye is winging wide across the light
to where the border into Scotland lies
below, and that cloud there, he's sailing – sail to France
and say hello to all my memories
from me, down here, a captive – journey well
your road is yours – you're free in air
no queens you can be subject to up there

KENNEDY   My lady, sweetheart, please – look over there:
they're spies. We're being watched. I don't like it
they've cleared the park so that we're here alone

MARY   You're wrong – believe me – that's not it *at all*
that they've unlocked my prison is a sign
that better things are coming – I'm not wrong
it's Leicester – somehow – has a hand in this
and now my prison walls will widen out – and out

and we will be more free with every inch
until we see that face – and we're *released*

KENNEDY   It just doesn't make sense. First thing today
            they sentence you to death; and now you're free
            it gives me a strange feeling, something's wrong

MARY   Listen – the hunt is coming – that's the horn
            that mellow swelling golden sound – their hooves
            cast up the dust in clouds – and press the grass
            the memories – the memories – the joy

Enter PAULET.

PAULET   Now! Do I deserve a 'thank you'?

MARY   Was this *you*?

PAULET   I did just as you asked me. Happy now?

MARY   The letter? I'm here because she read the letter?

PAULET   It was delivered as per your request.

MARY   And now I'm free

PAULET   That's not the only thing

MARY   What do you mean?

PAULET   You must have heard those horns.
            The Queen is hunting in this park.

MARY   The Queen?

PAULET   And any moment now she stands before you.

MARY is shaking.

KENNEDY   What's wrong, my lady?

PAULET   This *was* your request
            your wish was granted faster than you thought
            well, now's the time: you're good with words
            this is your time to speak

MARY You should have *warned me*
Now! I'm not prepared! I can't – not now
my best wish terrifies me now – Hanna,
I need to go inside – recover / there and

PAULET Stand still
You wait here and you meet Her Majesty.
You must be frightened – on your terms, of course,
it's finally time for you to face a judge

Enter TALBOT, running.

MARY It's not because of that – Talbot, help me
I cannot meet the Queen today – the sight
is more than I can bear

TALBOT Control yourself
This meeting will determine everything

MARY I hoped – I waited – years and years and years –
rehearsing what I'd say, and how I'd act
the words I'd use to cut right to her heart
and fill her full of empathy and pity:
forgotten – all of it – like *that* – and and and and
everything *lost* and nothing lives in me,
not now, *except* a white-hot hatred – swells
rearing up the kingdom of my soul
to *war* against the way she's treated me

TALBOT Stop it
bottle your rage – when hate meets hate
the outcome's never good. Control yourself
obey the time – obey the situation
she has the power over you – *submit*

MARY Submit – queen to a queen? I can't – I *can't*

TALBOT *YOU HAVE NO CHOICE!* So, speak respectfully
submission is the only role you've got
so play it *well* – let her be generous

,

MARY   I've pulled my own destruction down
              heavy on my head – and neck – the two of us,
              Elizabeth and me – we should not meet
              we should not *ever* meet. And if we do
              it will be violent – what do you expect
              when flame meets water – [or] tiger meets a lamb
              I am too deeply hurt – so badly hurt
              and hurt *by her* – peace is impossible

TALBOT   I watched her while she read your letter – tears
              in her eyes – it shook her into pity
              The queen has human feelings – just be *brave*
              I ran ahead so I could say: be calm

              MARY takes TALBOT's hand.

MARY   Yes – oh you're a friend to me – I wish
              they hadn't transferred me from you
              and your kind, heartfelt care –

TALBOT   Forget that now
              and set your mind to pure subservience

MARY   Is Burleigh with her too, my evil angel?

TALBOT   It's only Leicester with her –

MARY   Leicester?

TALBOT   Yes
              but don't be scared – it's Leicester was the one
              who got the Queen to meet you face to face.

MARY   I knew he would

TALBOT   What do you mean?

PAULET   The Queen

              *Everyone moves to the side. KENNEDY holds MARY to her.
              Then, ELIZABETH enters with LEICESTER – and as they approach:*

ELIZABETH What do they call this castle?

LEICESTER   Fotheringay

69

ELIZABETH looks at LEICESTER – and then at MARY.

The two of them are now on the same stage. It should feel as if something has completed: we're waiting for the two chemicals to react.

ELIZABETH My people's love for me can be excessive
a god deserves such honour: not a man.

MARY for the first time turns her face to ELIZABETH. Their eyes meet – and hold.

Who is the Lady?

,

LEICESTER   My Queen, we are at Fotheringay –

MARY is shaking. ELIZABETH, darkly:

ELIZABETH Who is responsible for this?

,

[SPEAK,] *Lord Leicester!*

LEICESTER Well – it has happened, Majesty – and since
your God has led you here – be merciful
Your Majesty, let your compassion reign

TALBOT Your Majesty, I beg you graciously to look
on the unlucky woman who stands before you

ELIZABETH Well, everyone?

,

Who was it told me she was deeply humbled?
She's proud. Not beaten down by her misfortune.

MARY Let that be.
I will forget now who I am – and what
I've suffered. I bow my self before you.

MARY kneels before ELIZABETH.

God fought on your side, sister. You have won.
Your crown – your victory – is at the height,
I honour you, Elizabeth, your highness
and honour most of all the highest King.
Now be my sister in compassion – offer
your hand and lift me up from where I've fallen.

ELIZABETH   You are where you belong, Lady Mary.
It's God who makes you kneel to me, and God
decrees that I shall never kneel to you.

MARY's emotions are rising, but she keeps it together –

MARY   Remember everything can change. Remember that.
And arrogance is punished by the gods
they cast me at your feet – to be *your test*,
not mine, in front of every person here,
honour your name and your royal blood, which runs
in both our veins – Oh God – *be merciful*
my all, my life, a woman's life now hangs
on what I say – my life is in my words
if I can make you see that I *am* you:
I am just as you are – let me *express* that,
but when you look at me like this, all ice
I'm choked – I'm terrified – no words can come

ELIZABETH is cold and severe.

ELIZABETH   I thought you had something to say to me.
You asked us for this meeting – we put by
all of your crimes against us, our role as Queen
and came – to do the duty of a sister,
to bring you comfort in our presence here,
and grant your wish – but by stooping so low,
by yielding to our generous impulses,
we have exposed our crown to public shame
to meet someone who would have murdered us –

MARY   I have something to say – but – I don't know
I don't know where to start. My words must pierce
your heart but never graze your skin – I mean

I mean you no offence – nothing in me
is trying to make you angry – but in my case – that is
to speak my case at all is to indict you. So
I ask God to give force to what I say – but
strip from my words the thorns of slight or harm
and let me tell the simple truth: you have
not treated me as I deserved – we are,
we are *both queens*. And you imprisoned me.
I came here as a suppliant and you
ignoring basic hospitality
throwing aside all international law
you locked me up, you tore my friends from me,
cruelly removed my servants, hauled me up in court,
that trial, that indefensible, illegal trial –
but no – *enough* – these things must be forgotten
Oblivion will shrink them into dust
I'll say that it was chance – that it was fate
not *your* fault – and not *my* fault, just the way
things happened. Let's let that be history.
We both know that this started long ago
and some black demon planted seeds of hate
when we were young – that swelled into *this* – now
and evil men have fed that, fanned its flames
until this *chasm* gapes between us now
and mad extremists push us to the brink –
but then the curse of every single king
is that our private feelings aren't our own
they magnify – and cleave the world in half
and in the gap between pure hate pours in
burning like ice – but no third parties now
no, now at last we're standing face to face
so speak to me – and name my crime
and I'll reply – I'll answer every charge
I'll satisfy you on the smallest point – my God
I wish you'd let me meet you years ago
I wish you'd let me look into your eyes
we never would have come to this today

ELIZABETH   My better angels saved me from the snake
from bringing it so close to my own skin.
You can't blame fate. Look at your own black heart
the wild ambition of your poisonous house:
between us, there was no hostility
at all – but then your uncle declared war
persuaded you to use my coat of arms
and sign your name as England's Royal Queen
you sought my death – enlisting godless priests
and rabid frenzied cults to light their brands
you goaded other nations' grudges, even *here*
you tried to rip apart *this* nation's peace
but God fights on my side – and He ensures
your uncle's war is dead – and here we are:
the blade you aimed at my neck swings back round
and slashes into yours

MARY   I'm in God's hands
you will not wield your power so bloodily

ELIZABETH   And who is going to stop me? Is it *you*?
What is your 'international law' to me?
And what is family? What is 'royal blood'?
If we are so alike – then how about
I follow the example of your Church
that makes killing a queen a holy act
and practise simply what your own priests preach?
There's not a single promise you can make
that I can trust – how can I set you free?
On what book can you swear? 'Cause there's no lock
that Catholic treachery won't unpick. *Speak up!*

,

Yes, as I thought. Our security is *force.*
And we will not negotiate with *snakes.*

MARY   Oh that is your suspicious paranoia!
You treated me as your enemy from the start
and as the *other* – and ignored my claim,
and how you look at something's what it *is*:

if you had simply named me as your heir
which I have every right to ask of you
I would have been your truest friend – and family

ELIZABETH Your family's over there in Catholic France!
The Pope's your friend! Name you my heir?
A trap – but telling: I'd sit there, alive
while you seduce my people – with your eyes
and throw your nets out for our younger men
so they all turn to the new-rising sun
while I –

MARY   would rule in peace! Listen: here and now
all claims to England's throne I abdicate
I let them go – *ach* – my spirit's wings
are broken, lame – I do not feel the lure
of greatness. You've achieved it. I am –
I am only Mary Stuart's shadow.
You locked me up for years – my spirit's dead
you've done your worst – to catch me at my height
and crush me down to nothing – make it end
finish this – and say the thing you came
to say: I don't believe you came to taunt me:
just say the words – please say the words – you're free
Mary, you've felt my power until now – today
you feel my mercy' – say that and I will beg
my self, my life, my freedom and my crown
from your royal hand as gifts – just *say the words*
and none of this has happened – say the words
but please don't make me wait – say one word – sister
I fear for you if you can leave this park
not having blessed me. I don't *want* your power
I wouldn't take it for your entire kingdom – not
for all the earth and water on the globe

ELIZABETH So you confess – at last – you are defeated?
There's no more plots? And no more murderers
are on their way? no martyrs for your cause?
Yes – that's it, Lady Mary – you're old news.
There's no one left you can seduce – the world

has other things to think about – you're *done*.
No man is begging to be husband number four
though then that's not surprising – as we know,
your husbands – like your lovers – end up dead

MARY   Sister – oh God – let me control myself

ELIZABETH's eyes are bright and sharp, genuinely sexually triumphant:

ELIZABETH So this, Lord Leicester – *this* is the beauty
so dangerous that men fell with one glance
and earthly women just could not compete.
Really. It seems *that* reputation's cheap:
but then – it's true – the crowds *would* praise your charms
when you've had half of them between your sheets

MARY   *Too much –*

ELIZABETH   And now her mask slips, now we see
her face – her own true self

MARY glows with anger – but holds her dignity, just.

MARY   My sins were *human* ones
and I was young – I made mistakes – it's true
power seduced me, yes, I don't deny it:
instead of fabricating public lies
I chose the *honesty* that becomes a crown
I let the worst be known – and I can say
that I am greater than my reputation is.
But once they rip your ermine cloak away
once this façade of virtue falls apart
the world will see exactly what you are
the red hot fires of your secret lusts –
the Virgin Queen? just like your mother, then!
Control the way they write about it – fine! –
but that won't make it true – everyone *knows*
the reason Anne Boleyn was put to death

Something breaks in ELIZABETH.

TALBOT   No – it cannot come to this – control yourself

MARY   There comes a point where it is inhumane
             where any human would explode – would burst
             the walls – the anger rushes out like blood
             I wish my words could *kill* you – murder you
             slice out your *eyes*

Things have reached the point of no return.

TALBOT   She is beside herself
             she's mad, your majesty – she needs your *help* /
             and not your condemnation

LEICESTER in huge anxiety tries to lead a speechless ELIZABETH away.

LEICESTER   Let's go – don't listen to her frenzy – come away

MARY   The Queen of England is a bastard Queen
             your throne's defiled, this honest country is
             the victim of a con – *you* [Elizabeth] are a fraud
             a thief – *imposter* – and if right prevailed
             you'd bow before me honouring my right
             you would be lying prostrate in the dust
             I AM YOUR KING

ELIZABETH exits, swiftly – followed by the train.

KENNEDY   What are you doing?
             She's furious – [she's] leaving – our hopes are dead

MARY   'She's furious' – I hope her heart explodes
             I feel *well*, Hanna, finally – I can breathe
             after the years of shame – humiliation
             a single moment of pure victory
             A mountain's lifted off my chest – I stabbed
             a knife down deep into my enemy's stomach

KENNEDY   She's got the knife! You're mad! *She is the Queen*
             You slandered her – her lover heard it all

MARY   I humiliated her in front of Leicester
              He saw – he saw me win – my victory
              he gave me strength – he stood so near to me
              I climbed up and I beat her from her height

    MORTIMER runs in.

MORTIMER   *(To K.)* Make sure no one comes near
           (To M.)   I heard it all

    *KENNEDY takes her place on guard. MORTIMER's whole being is
    suppressing a huge wave of ferocious, excited passion. Though he might
    first appear comic, there's something increasingly frightening about
    him – as this conversation progresses.*

              You've won. You *won* – you stamped them into dust
              They were the criminals – you were the Queen
              the *courage* of you – you are a *goddess*

MARY   Did you give him my letter – Leicester?

MORTIMER   Your anger *blazed* – it shone like holy light – you are
           the most beautiful woman in the world

MARY   Did you give him my letter? Is there *hope*?

MORTIMER   There is – but not from Leicester. He's a coward.

MARY   What?

MORTIMER   If he wants to rescue you – then first
              he'll have to fight me to the death

MARY   *LISTEN*
              Did Leicester get my letter?

MORTIMER   Leicester likes his life
              to save you now a man must love his *death*

MARY   Is Leicester going to save me?

MORTIMER   No, he's not.
              We don't need him. I'm saving you.

MARY   *(Sarcastic.)*   With *what*?

MORTIMER Stop lying to yourself. You're wasting time.
Your case, this situation's crossed a line
and how things were this morning? Dead and gone.
Elizabeth left – and then – so did the chance
of her showing you mercy – it's time to *act*
we have to be audacious – and this fight
is now. We break you out of here tonight.

MARY Impossible

MORTIMER No – it's happening – listen
we came together secretly today
we made confession to a Catholic priest
who absolved us of our sins – and future sins
(knowing your rescue will be dearly bought)
but we took our last sacrament – and we
are ready now to start on our last journey

MARY I can't hear this

MORTIMER You know I'm jailer now
The Queen put me in charge of you – and so
I have the keys. We blow open the walls
we kill the guards and take you from your room
tonight

MARY You kill the guards?

MORTIMER No other way
we can't leave witnesses to your escape

MARY And Paulet? And the guards? They're going to fight.

MORTIMER We kill them first.

MARY Kill your own uncle?

MORTIMER Yes

MARY The crime of / murder's heavy

MORTIMER murder's pardoned in advance
Some things have to be done. And I am ready.
I want it to come.

MARY   No – no –

MORTIMER   And if tonight
                     my knife must split the windpipe of the Queen
                     if that is what God wants – I swore on Jesus' blood
                     that I would do it

MARY   Too much blood for me –

MORTIMER   I'd give the world and everything for you
                     I love you – let the structure of the globe
                     dissolve and start a giant foaming wave
                     to flood the lungs of everything that breathes
                     There's *nothing* I respect – the end of days
                     will come before I let them put their hands
                     on you

MARY   You're frightening me

MORTIMER   Life is over quickly
                     so is death – let them restrain me, carry me to Tyburn
                     pull out my joints and flesh and burn my skin
                     let them bring red-hot knives – life does not *last*
                     I need to touch you now

MARY   Get away from me

MORTIMER   I want to taste your skin, your hands, your mouth
                     they're going to kill you – you're *already dead*
                     your white neck severed with a heavy axe
                     I'll hold them back – I'll kill a *thousand souls*
                     I'll rescue you – I will – and I will *have* you
                     God put you purposely into my hand – *you're mine*
                     I want to be inside you

MARY   Listen – *please*
                     respect me as a woman and a queen
                     my grief – my situation – and my crown

MORTIMER   There's no crown on your head. It's fallen off.
                     You have no power. You can't give commands.
                     Your body is the only thing that's left

you're you – your hair – your body – just a *girl*
but that's enough – for that I dare do *everything*
it drives me toward death

MORTIMER's eyes are wild – he is going to rape her if needs be.

MARY   I do not want this
I'll tell them all you're here to rescue me

MORTIMER COME ON – you're not like her – the frigid queen
I've heard the stories – Darnley and Bothwell

MARY   How dare you say his name

MORTIMER   Bothwell! I dare.
He was a bully – your love was soaked in fear
but maybe fear's the thing you understand

MARY   Let me go – *HELP*

KENNEDY runs back in, terrified, but not at this attempted rape –

Hanna, I –

*And suddenly PAULET and other men are running into the scene –
MARY is wrestled to the floor and gagged.*

PAULET   Where is the murderer? The gates are *shut*
Where is the Scottish queen? Don't move an inch –
Take hold of her – restrain her – now now now

MORTIMER Uncle? What's happening?

PAULET   Get the criminal
inside the prison – you do not leave her door
or even *blink* – without my saying so. Admit no one else

*PAULET looks at his nephew, wild-eyed – in shock, emotional, perhaps
tearful – voice trembling – something is very, very wrong…*

MORTIMER What's GOING ON?

PAULET   The Queen – oh God – the Queen

MORTIMER The Queen? Which Queen?

He can hardly believe he's saying the words.

PAULET   Elizabeth –
was murdered as she travelled back to London

,

Everyone exits, fast, different doors –

INTERVAL.

ACT FOUR

MORTIMER enters swiftly, pacing, thinking, then BURLEIGH and DAVISON enter – everyone adrenalized.

BURLEIGH   Draw up the execution warrant *now*.
            Get on with it. The second it's complete
            it goes before the Queen for her to sign.

MORTIMER   Sir, is the Queen alive?

BURLEIGH   Shocked – but alive

DAVISON   Lord Talbot saved her life – the madman's blade
            glanced off the shoulder of the Queen – but missed
            and then Lord Talbot [forced him to the ground]

BURLEIGH   Thank you, Davison
            Your duty isn't journalism. Go.

> *DAVISON exits.*

MORTIMER   Who attacked her?

BURLEIGH   A Catholic radical,
            a priest – he's French – we're questioning him now.
            The Pope had excommunicated her
            so murder was fair game – and they moved fast
            to liberate the Catholic church.

> *Enter LEICESTER. BURLEIGH ignores him.*

LEICESTER   The park's locked down.

> *Enter AUBESPINE, out of breath –*

AUBESPINE   Praise be to God that he has saved the Queen

BURLEIGH   Praise be to God that crushed her enemies

AUBESPINE   May God condemn whoever did this deed

BURLEIGH   The puppet and whoever pulled the strings

AUBESPINE turns to LEICESTER.

AUBESPINE My lord, please grant me access to the Queen
                  I wish to lay my lord the King's support,
                  and France's thoughts and prayers, down at her feet

BURLEIGH Don't waste your breath, Lord Aubespine

AUBESPINE, officially:

AUBESPINE Respect, Lord Burleigh, I have a duty here.

BURLEIGH Your duty is to go back home to France
               as soon as possible.

AUBESPINE   I don't understand –

BURLEIGH The status of 'ambassador' keeps you safe
               today – but not tomorrow

AUBESPINE   On what *grounds*?

BURLEIGH I'm sure you don't want me to name your crime

AUBESPINE My rights as France's royal ambassador / will –

BURLEIGH will not protect a traitor to our Queen.

LEICESTER Burleigh, what is this?

AUBESPINE   My lord, think carefully
               before you –

BURLEIGH A passport with your signature on was found
               on the assassin's person.

       ,

AUBESPINE I authorise many passports, sir. I don't read minds.

BURLEIGH The assassin made confession at your home.

AUBESPINE I am a Catholic and my home is open

BURLEIGH to every anti-English maniac?

AUBESPINE Lord Burleigh, I demand a full inquiry

BURLEIGH   Careful what you wish for

AUBESPINE   The French King will be furious
to hear how you have treated him – through me.
The marriage treaty will be reconsidered.

BURLEIGH   The Queen's already torn it up. For good.
The English crown will not be marrying France.

     ,

*BURLEIGH has a piece of paper handed to him. Looks almost amused,
quizzical.*

The people are incensed. They've stormed your house
and found stockpiles of weapons hidden there.
I'll grant you your immunity until
you're off our soil – safe conduct and your life,
that's more than you can reasonably ask.

AUBESPINE   To leave a country that ignores the laws
that unite half the world – will be my pleasure.
Your royal court's a playground – and the King
will force your Queen to pay the price for this

BURLEIGH   Well, he can come and ask for it himself

AUBESPINE leaves.

LEICESTER   The wedding suit with France is over, then.
You built it up – and now you knock it down,
Lord Burleigh. Keeping busy all the time.
No benefits to England, though – a shame!
you might as well have saved yourself the trouble.

BURLEIGH   I did what I thought best. God disagreed.
If only every man could say the same.

LEICESTER   Be honest, you enjoy all this. Good time
for you – you've got someone to hunt,
a major incident – but the criminals' guilt
wrapped up in secrecy – and so we need
a court of inquisition! Weighing looks

and words – exhibiting private *thoughts*
to public view: and Burleigh reigns supreme!
the number one, the Atlas of our times
on his shoulders the safety of the state.

BURLEIGH   I've got a lot to learn from you, Lord Leicester:
your way with words won quite the victory

LEICESTER   What victory?

BURLEIGH   Your trip to Fotheringay.
The one you talked the Queen into behind
my back.

LEICESTER   Behind your back! And why would I
need to conceal something from you, my Lord?

BURLEIGH   You led the Queen to Fotheringay – I'm sorry
that's not quite right – the thing I meant to say
is that your Queen led *you* to Fotheringay.

LEICESTER is unsettled. What does BURLEIGH know?

BURLEIGH speaks with smooth, sharp confidence.

LEICESTER   If I were you, I would explain myself –

BURLEIGH   A very noble role you had her play,
the Queen – she trusts you, clearly – gullibly
and in return she's made a mockery of.
But that *was* why you came on merciful
before the council (quite the change of heart)
and quite the way with words: the Stuart *weak*
and insignificant – not to be feared
and barely worth the trouble of her death.
Good plan. Well, sharp. Well, sharpened to a point.
A shame the point snapped off.

LEICESTER   Say that again
say that again before the Queen.

BURLEIGH   I will
Let's see your way with words protect you then.

Exit BURLEIGH. LEICESTER alone.

LEICESTER   He's onto me. Seen through me. If there's proof
I'm finished – if they know Mary and I
have understandings – God, there's no way out
she'll think I gave her dishonest advice
betrayed her to her oldest enemy
persuaded her to go to Fotheringay
it all looks like a *plan!* Oh Christ in heaven
she'll think that Mary's anger was an act
and even the assassin – no escape
from how they'll read events – no mercy then:
I'm finished.

MORTIMER enters, terrified, looks around apprehensively.

MORTIMER   Leicester – are we alone?

LEICESTER   Look: go away.

MORTIMER   They're on my track
and they're on yours.

LEICESTER   GET OUT OF HERE

MORTIMER   They know there was a secret meeting at
the French Ambassador's house –

LEICESTER   Why would I *care*?
I've had / enough

MORTIMER   They know the assassin was there

LEICESTER   That was *your* plan
don't implicate me in your dirty crimes

MORTIMER   Just *listen*

LEICESTER   Die in hell. I don't *know* you.

LEICESTER in violent anger is leaving, when –

MORTIMER   I came to *warn* you. They know everything.

LEICESTER   What?

MORTIMER   Lord Burleigh got to Fotheringay at once
just minutes after everything had happened
they searched her rooms – Queen Mary's rooms – they found
a letter

LEICESTER   what?

MORTIMER   a letter that the Queen
was writing to you

LEICESTER   no – *the STUPID WOMAN*

MORTIMER   in which she calls on you to keep your word – and
renews the promise of her hand in marriage

LEICESTER   *God*

MORTIMER   Lord Burleigh has that letter

                  ,

LEICESTER   And *goodnight.*

*LEICESTER retches, perhaps. As MORTIMER speaks, LEICESTER thinks
hard –*

MORTIMER   Be brave – and seize the moment. Now. Before
Lord Burleigh does – you can save her
and save yourself – invent excuses, swear
anything to get you out of this.
Our men are scattered – nothing I can do
the whole thing's blown wide open – I'll escape
to Scotland, bring our cause to order there.
But here, it's up to you. Be ruthless. Think.
See what your influence can do. Good luck.
Be *bold.*

LEICESTER stops walking – totally still.

LEICESTER   You're right.

He calls out of the door.

                  Hey – hey – HEY – GUARDS!

KENT enters.

This man's a traitor to the state.
He's just confessed his plot against the Queen
(To M.) In the Queen's name, you are under arrest.
(To K.) You guard the door. I'll call more men – and then
I'll take the news into the Queen myself.

*LEICESTER exits, quickly. KENT stands at the doorway, preventing
MORTIMER from getting away.*

MORTIMER is astonished –

MORTIMER   The bastard. But this is what I deserve
for trusting him. And he took my advice:
betraying me builds him a bridge – and he
walks free on top of it. And leaves me to
the wolves.

*MORTIMER has the means of suicide on him: perhaps a tablet, taken
from a small silver box. He's been prepared for this from the start.*

But I won't do the same to him – my fall
won't try to bring him down: my lips are sealed.
This world is nothing – my eyes look to heaven
my freedom is my soul – and I ask God
to curse these men who turn from the true Queen
Queen Mary Stuart – and with my last breath
I love you – we two will be one in death

*MORTIMER takes the tablet. And when KENT re-enters – MORTIMER
is dead.*

*Enter ELIZABETH – her shirt is bloodied, partially ripped. There is
a letter in her hand. BURLEIGH follows after her.*

ELIZABETH   To take me to that park – to laugh at me
make me perform in front of his vile whore
you *stupid woman*, tricked, betrayed and shamed!

BURLEIGH   Your Majesty, I don't know what he did
to work his way around your royal wisdom –

ELIZABETH　He's laughing at me. I went to taunt *her*
but she – and he – humiliated *me.*
I'll swing the axe into her neck myself

BURLEIGH　You see now *my* advice was accurate

ELIZABETH　I should have listened: we wouldn't be *here*
oh I trusted him – I shouldn't have trusted him
and all his vows he loved me – they were traps?
Who can I trust when even he betrayed me?
I let him play the King within this court
he wormed inside my heart, trussed up my soul

BURLEIGH　But all that time he was duplicitous:
betraying you to Mary Queen of Scots.
the letter in your hand confirms the truth.

ELIZABETH　They'll pay for this. In blood. Have you drawn up
the death warrant?

BURLEIGH　　　　　　　　　They're doing it as we speak.

ELIZABETH　I want her dead. I want her DEAD. All right:
She dies. He watches. Then he dies himself.
(She roars.)
I'll rip him from my heart, I'll spit him out
and every fingerful of flesh that felt his love
I'll slice it out and fill it with *revenge*
You fall from high up – and you break. And he
was high – enough! – drag him to the Tower
I'll name the peers to sentence him, and he
will face the full force of the law.

BURLEIGH　He'll try and talk to you –

ELIZABETH　　　　　　　　　What can he say?
This letter casts its argument in stone.
His crime is clear as day

BURLEIGH　　　　　　　　You're merciful
and seeing him, it's possible / you'll [think again]

89

ELIZABETH   I will not *ever* set eyes on him again.
Nemesis... You gave the order barring him?

BURLEIGH   I did.

ELIZABETH   Wait here – and when he comes, arrest him.

Enter KENT.

KENT   Your Majesty, Lord Leicester is outside

ELIZABETH   He can't come in. Get out and tell him that.

KENT   Your Majesty, I would not dare say that
to Leicester – he won't accept that from me

ELIZABETH   My subjects fear his anger more than mine

BURLEIGH   Tell him the Queen denies him access

BURLEIGH gestures for KENT to go – ELIZABETH signals him to pause –

ELIZABETH   This couldn't be – a trap that *Mary* set
words on a page designed to draw me in
and cut Lord Leicester down at the same time?

BURLEIGH   But think, Your Majesty / consider

Enter LEICESTER, fast, sees BURLEIGH.

LEICESTER   I might have guessed that this was down to you
if you'll see Burleigh, you can see me too

BURLEIGH   It's pretty brave to storm in here when you've
explicitly been forbidden by the Queen

LEICESTER   It's brave of *you* to try and keep me out
there's *no one* at this court who has the right
to tell the Earl of Leicester where he can
and cannot go. From my own Queen, I want / to hear

He has approached ELIZABETH, who does not look at him.

ELIZABETH   Out of my sight

LEICESTER   Those aren't your words
Lord Burleigh put them in your mouth, but I
want *yours*, my own gracious Elizabeth
talk to me, let me explain – as you let him
put his malicious story

ELIZABETH   Go ahead
Deny your crime. Perjure yourself. Go on.

LEICESTER   Let your officious watchman leave the room
before we speak – Burleigh, get out –
My Queen and I do not require a witness.

ELIZABETH   He stays. By my command.

LEICESTER   Elizabeth
when have we ever needed anyone else?
This is between the two of us – send him out.
I have the right to talk to you alone –

ELIZABETH   Do you indeed?

LEICESTER   You made me what I am
lifted me up – and trusted me – and *more* –
your heart gave me whatever honour I have
I will defend that honour with my life
Two minutes. Send him out. And hear me speak.

ELIZABETH   No silky words will talk you out of this.

LEICESTER   I only want to speak straight to your heart
explain my actions – what I've done and why
how I relied on our relationship
to take the risks I've taken: my defence
is only to be judged by your own heart
and not by any of Lord Burleigh's courts

ELIZABETH   Shameless.
Lord Burleigh, please. Show him the letter.

*BURLEIGH hands the letter over. LEICESTER skim-reads it. His face
doesn't change at all – not a single flicker of surprise.*

LEICESTER It's Mary Stuart's writing.

ELIZABETH   Read it *silently*.

    LEICESTER finishes reading it.

LEICESTER I know that this looks bad, but there is more
than simply how things look

ELIZABETH   Can you deny
that you've had secret contact with the Stuart
and Catholic networks plotting her escape?

LEICESTER If I *were* guilty, I'd claim this was fake,
my enemies at Court had set me up
but – my conscience is *clear* – and what she writes
is true

ELIZABETH   That isn't good, is it?

BURLEIGH   He's just
pronounced his death sentence himself

ELIZABETH Enough. Escort Lord Leicester to the Tower.

LEICESTER I was working for *you* – I got it wrong
I should have told you everything – but still
I won her confidence only so we'd know
the details and could *sabotage* her plan

ELIZABETH This is absurd

BURLEIGH   Sir, do you *really* think / that

LEICESTER Yes – I've played a dangerous game. I know.
And no one else at court would have presumed
to risk so much – but God, I love my Queen
I *knew* her faith in me would guarantee
this high-risk strategy – which was worth the risk
because, in fact, it has now saved her life.
They'd tried to kill the Queen three times – and look,
the honours I've received from her, my rank
they don't suggest much motive to defect
and you – and you – and all the world has heard
how deep my hatred is for Mary Stuart –

BURLEIGH   So if your plan's so great, why keep it secret?

LEICESTER   My lord, you love to talk before you act
ringing the bell before you get things done
That's your way. This is mine: *talk afterwards.*

BURLEIGH   You're talking now to save your skin.

LEICESTER   And you
have come in here to boast that you, again,
have done a great fantastic brilliant deed
uncovered plots, rescued Her Majesty
exposed the treachery to all. *Ironically*
you think that you see everything, that you
don't miss a trick – but, sad to say, you *do*
because – despite your boasting – Mary Stuart
would now be free, had I not been alert.

BURLEIGH   Are you really claiming – ?

LEICESTER   *Yes.* Let me explain.
Lord Burleigh, I know much more than you think.
I know the Queen had trusted Mortimer,
revealed her private wishes, ordered him
to murder Mary Stuart in her cell –
a task which horrified his uncle Paulet
who had refused to do it

BURLEIGH   Who told you that?

LEICESTER   It *is* the truth, correct me if I'm wrong?
Exactly. Other people do see things.
Not you, though, Burleigh – you managed to miss
the hundred clues that Mortimer was *false*
and Catholic and a murderous radical
fighting in secret on the Stuart's *side,*
determined – yes – to kill the Queen, but not
the Scottish one – *Elizabeth!*

ELIZABETH   Lord Mortimer!

LEICESTER   He was the one who brought the Stuart's letters.
That's how I came to know him first. He said

minutes ago – they planned to break her out
tonight – by force – to take her from her cell –
I broke my cover and revealed myself
and called the guards – put him under arrest
but knowing he was trapped with no way out,
without a warning, he has killed himself –

ELIZABETH is hit hard by this new bad news.

ELIZABETH   Betrayed again. The seeds were poisoned too
and so we reap this poisoned harvest now –

BURLEIGH   This happened now? After I'd left the room?

LEICESTER   I wish he wasn't dead – not least because
his testimony would prove my innocence.
That's why I broke my cover when I did.

BURLEIGH   He killed himself, you say? It wasn't you?

LEICESTER   That question isn't worthy of you. Go ask Kent
he will corroborate everything I've said

ELIZABETH   Oh this is hell

LEICESTER   So who has saved the Queen?
Was it Lord Burleigh? Did he know the danger
converging round your Majesty today?
Where was *his* plan? Which of us served you best?
Who was the faithful angel to his Queen?

BURLEIGH   Mortimer's death came right on time for you

ELIZABETH   I don't know what to say – I believe you
and I don't – You're guilty – and you're not.
And the mother of this hell is Mary Stuart
I say 'we are the Queen' – '*we* are': *we are*
'we are the Queen' – the *two of us* are queen:
I wear the crown, but she holds all the cards
for years her secret influence – seeps in
like woodworm hollowing out our government
and leaving us a husk of what we are
her prison cell's the centre of the state
and tension settles thick round us, like snow

LEICESTER   She has to die. I ask for it myself.
            Remember what I said in council – that
            the blade falls when the uprising begins?
            The uprising's begun. The blade should fall.

BURLEIGH   Lord Leicester, you're the one –

LEICESTER   Please let's be clear:
            the safety of her Majesty is paramount
            today has proved they want to end her life
            let's not wait for their next attempt. Extreme
            measures are called for. Execute the sentence.

            ,

BURLEIGH   So confident – so serious, and so honest
            surely Lord Leicester is the perfect man
            to bear the burden of this crucial act?
            perhaps assign the doing of this to him?

LEICESTER   To me?

BURLEIGH   To you. How better to destroy
            all the suspicion buzzing around your name?
            No one will dare suggest you were in love
            when you're the man that has her put to death.

            ELIZABETH fixes her eyes on LEICESTER.

ELIZABETH   That's shrewd advice. So ordered.

LEICESTER   Elizabeth
            my standing in the court makes me unfit
            for such a gory office. Surely it's best
            that Burleigh is responsible – he's not
            so close to you – to the public, then, it's not
            the crown, but the judicial system, which
            takes Mary's life. But if you wish me to,
            I'll prove my love, I'll waive my privileges
            and show my loyalty – I'll accept the task.

ELIZABETH   You're right.
            Burleigh can share responsibility

with you. You're equals now. So get it done.
I want the warrant here *immediately*.

BURLEIGH exits.

ELIZABETH and LEICESTER alone.

Then KENT enters, a bit shaken.

KENT   Your Majesty there's crowds outside the palace.
              They want to see your face.

ELIZABETH   What's going on?

KENT   Panic has spread – the rumour that you've died
              has travelled fast – but even then they won't
              they don't trust what we're telling them
              they know the Catholics move against your life
              and that they'll strike to break the Stuart free
              the crowds are furious and terrified

ELIZABETH   Is there suggestion they'll turn violent?
              What do they want?

KENT   They want the Stuart's head.
              They won't leave till the death warrant is signed.

              *BURLEIGH re-enters with DAVISON, who has the warrant in his
              hands.*

ELIZABETH   Are you aware my people are outside?

BURLEIGH   We are.

              *DAVISON puts down the death warrant. The sheer size of what it
              represents is overwhelming. Everyone looks at it. ELIZABETH hesitates
              – fighting with herself.*

ELIZABETH   Oh God

BURLEIGH   Your Majesty, obey the people's voice. It is
              the voice of God

              BURLEIGH takes the lid off a pen, offers it to her.

,

Pressure beats in ELIZABETH's ears – she's a trapped animal.

ELIZABETH   And which man here will guarantee me *now*
I hear the voice of all my people, *all*
who stand on England's soil – *no*, on the world?
Is this decision *really* what they want?
'Cause I'm afraid that, once I sign this thing
once I obey the people's lust for death –
then we'll all hear a different, darker voice
and everyone who now wants this thing done
will turn against me as a murderer

Enter TALBOT, as KENT runs back outside.

TALBOT   Don't let them rush you into this, Your Majesty,
take time – stand firm

He sees the death warrant.

                            Has it already happened?
Get that disgusting piece of paper out
of here – Your Majesty, tear it up –

ELIZABETH   What can I do? They're forcing me

TALBOT   Who is?
No man can force the Queen of England's hand.
You're Queen. Command your people to *shut up*.
How dare they threaten you? They're blind and scared
and you're still reeling – you have been attacked
today! You're only human. Suspend judgement.

BURLEIGH   It's already been *judged* – sentence was passed
in court: the *execution* of the sentence
is all that's left.

KENT re-enters. New news. Tenser and tenser.

KENT   It's getting worse out there. The uproar swells
we're told it's getting hard to hold it down

ELIZABETH   They're pushing me and pushing me

TALBOT   Push back

Postpone the thing – tell them you want to *wait*
You sign that paper – that's your legacy
your life, your peace, your happiness – the lot.
You've been debating this for *years* – this storm
is not the place to make a snap decision.
Ask for a pause. Collect your thoughts. And breathe.

BURLEIGH   *(Violently.)* Yes, breathe, while London crackles into flames
take your time while the enemy regroups
four times now you've survived assassination
today's one by the fraction of a hair
perhaps you think these miracles are endless
to me, Your Majesty, it's tempting fate

TALBOT   It's a miracle God had this old man wrestle
the blade from your assassin's hands – you *are*
not going to die – your duty is to *God*
he won't forgive you if you murder her
against his will – and you can't wind it back

BURLEIGH   We've heard your case for her defence before

TALBOT   I'm not talking about justice – or the court
those arguments are out of place today
and in this turmoil – but listen to me
you're trembling now – and Mary Stuart *lives*
cut off her head, then everything gets worse
she's just a *problem* now: but when she's dead
her ghost, her story will chase you like a *wolf*
infecting hearts and minds – that hate her now
but once she's dead they'll rise up for revenge
the people in that crowd out there will *turn*
against you and your throne – they'll pity her
she won't be Catholic or their enemy then –
but just the victim of a tyrant Queen
a martyr – and you'll see how fast things change
travel through London when she's lost her head
wait for the jubilant crowds to greet you then
I know Lord Burleigh thirsts for Mary's blood
I know the crowds outside demand her death

and in your heart, there's part of *you* desires
to sign that paper, bring this to an end,
but Majesty, here's something else I know:
your people will desert you if you do
you'll push things past the limit: no one's head
is safe if Mary Stuart loses hers.

ELIZABETH   Talbot, you saved my life today. You know,
I wish you'd let me die. All this would *end.*
The blame, doubt, fear, morality – would stop
I would be lying, softening into earth.
Let's bring this to a head – and make it mine.
I'm tired of being Queen. I'm tired of life.
If how it has to be is: lose one queen
so one can live – and that's the only course
then – *please* – let me give in, collapse and grant
the crowds their wish, hand them the crown – oh God,
God is my witness: I have *only* lived
to serve the English people – but Mary Stuart
she offers them the hope of happier days
a younger queen – a better life – they can *have* her.
I'll leave the throne – live out in solitude
look up and see my England's soft green woods
as I did when I was young, and where I found
you see – now, I remember that – I found
the sort of deeper greatness in myself
that doesn't need a crown. I was not born
to be a queen – I'm not *not royal*
I have a heart – I'm soft – and and I have
I have ruled happily in happy times
but now? the first hard test: I'm powerless
weak

,

BURLEIGH   For *God's sake* – these unroyal words
I cannot tolerate them from your mouth
You say you love your people. Act for them.
If you don't serve them now, their lives are lost
Without you to protect them, what comes next?

The Catholic faith restored across your land
raping your subjects' souls – this is no time
for weakness or self pity: Majesty
England's immortal soul is in your hand
each one of them depends on your resolve
everything hangs on what you choose to do
Lord Talbot saved your life – now you save theirs

ELIZABETH Give me some time alone. No more advice
no counsel on the earth can help me now
I'll ask the higher monarch for his guidance.
Leave.

(To DAVISON.)   You – wait outside.

They all leave.

*As TALBOT exits, he looks pointedly at her – and then goes. ELIZABETH
is on her own. MARY is there too, but in ELIZABETH's thought.*

To serve the people is to be a slave.
I'm tired of flattering them, when – honestly –
I hate them. Really hate them. I have to respect
their unrefined opinions, their approval
and satisfy a fickle population:
the crown is just a prison cell with jewels.
There's only one way you can be a king:
it's having freedom to follow *your* will
without needing permission from the world.
I just want to be free and not tied up
You strive for justice, fairness, seeking balance
rejecting tyranny at every turn
then you look down – you've handcuffed your own wrists
But *have* I ruled like that from my free will?
even my virtues aren't really my *choice*:
they're things you have to be when you're a king.
Surrounded here by rings of enemies
public approval is the only thing
that keeps me on the throne – it's gone, I'm weak
and all the crowds have Mary in their hearts
while I'm reviled abroad – cursed by the Pope

the victim of this French false wedding trick
while Spain, sharpening its swords to slit my throat,
takes to the seas – meanwhile Queen Mary Stuart
sits in her cell, sits *smilingly*
sits waiting for history to hand her my crown
while I stand here alone – pulling my robes around me
to hide the shame that my claim to my throne
was stained by my own father – and my blood
my *birth* was shamefully laid bare as – as – *worth less*
and not fit for a queen. But *Mary Stuart*
my enemies claim her claim is sacrosanct
and so I am a woman on my own
naked against the world.
How can I ever truly wear the crown?

,

No – no – it *stops* – this terror has to end.
Your head will fall. This poison that infects
my life, my joy, my hope, my happiness
snatching my lovers – and my marriage plans
and beating through my reign, my time, my sleep –
and every single evil in my life –
has one hard, hated name: Mary Stuart
and once she is a corpse, I will be free
free and pure and clear as mountain air –

,

The way she looked at me. Like I was [nothing] –
There is a better weapon in my hand.
I use it and you die. You are no more.

ELIZABETH signs her name on the death warrant.

You worthless whore, you said I was a bastard?
I'll stop being a bastard when you're dead
and any doubt about my claim is gone
it's split in two as easily as your neck,
and blotted out as your head rolls in blood.
With no pretender left, I will be royal

by blood, by birth – and born to majesty

,

Davison –

DAVISON enters.

Where are the rest of them?

DAVISON   They've gone
          to calm the crowds. Lord Talbot went out first:
          they screamed and cheered that he had saved your life.

ELIZABETH   They change their mind with every breeze that blows,
          it's fatal to depend on them.

As if that was all she wanted, she dismisses DAVISON.

                                              Dismissed.
          And take this paper with you –

*DAVISON looks at the paper – is visibly shocked – this is huge. He's
hesitant, young, it's difficult for him to speak to the Queen without a
massive amount of anxiety.*

DAVISON   This is [signed] – your Majesty,
          You have decided?

ELIZABETH   They told me to sign,
          I signed. A piece of paper can't *decide.*
          A name can't kill.

DAVISON   Your name, your Majesty
          upon this piece of paper, *does* decide
          and kill – this is an execution warrant
          if you've signed this, then Mary Stuart dies
          your men will go to Fotheringay at once
          they will behead her now – before the dawn
          her life is over once this leaves the room

ELIZABETH   God has placed something crucial in your hands
          make sure you hear His wisdom. Do your duty.

She is about to leave the room.

DAVISON   No – your Majesty – don't leave – I'm sorry –
           I'm not sure what you're asking me to do
           can I be clear – you put this in my hands
           in order that its process will begin?

ELIZABETH I'm sure you're wise enough to work that out

           DAVISON talks quickly – he's terrified.

DAVISON   I'm not – no – please don't put this on my wisdom
           God forbid! I serve you – and obey your will
           and if I make a small mistake, she dies
           that's regicide – a huge catastrophe
           I'm just your instrument in this great cause
           just give me your instruction – in two words –
           what should I do with this death warrant?

ELIZABETH Its name makes that quite clear –

DAVISON   So you want execution carried out?

ELIZABETH My flesh crawls at that thought – I didn't say that

DAVISON   So I should just hold onto it?

ELIZABETH   If you do
           you'll face the consequences

DAVISON   I – ? For God's sake!
           Just give me your instruction – what do you want?

ELIZABETH I want to be alone. And I don't want
           to discuss this matter any more with you
           I want this finished now.

DAVISON   *Please* – one word
           tell me *exactly* what to do with this

ELIZABETH I've told you that already. You're dismissed.

DAVISON   You haven't told me anything? You've said
           nothing – Your Majesty, remember that –

ELIZABETH This is insufferable

DAVISON   Have pity on me
                    I'm new to this, I – I don't understand
                    the words or ways of court – I beg you, please
                    take back this paper! Take it from my hands!
                    It's white-hot flame – I do not wish to serve
                    your Majesty in this –

ELIZABETH   Just do your duty.

ELIZABETH leaves. DAVISON tearful, perhaps.

DAVISON   I don't know what that is.

BURLEIGH re-enters. DAVISON is terrified of him anyway.

                              I'm sorry, sir, I must
                    resign my office – I'm not cut out for this

BURLEIGH   I thought the Queen had summoned you inside?

DAVISON   She's angry – and she left

BURLEIGH   Where is the warrant?

DAVISON   It's here – she signed it – but she wouldn't / say –

BURLEIGH   It's signed? – then hand it over

DAVISON   No – I can't

BURLEIGH   What?

DAVISON   I have not had the order from the Queen

BURLEIGH   She signed it. That's an order. Give me it

DAVISON   I am to execute it – but hold onto it – and
                    not execute it – I don't know what to do
                    My life is [over] – *this decision can't be mine*

BURLEIGH   We execute it. Now. There isn't time.

BURLEIGH snatches the warrant from DAVISON's hands and exits.

ACT FIVE

The same room as ACT ONE. We've come full circle. The quiet atmosphere of a funeral – hanging in time. Death is present.

MELVIL enters: elderly, reliable, Scottish.

MELVIL   Ah, Hanna Kennedy, we meet again

KENNEDY   Are you – Melvil! I don't believe you're here
                    after this long, long, painful separation

MELVIL   Our reunion is a pretty painful one –

KENNEDY   Oh – then, you've come –

MELVIL   to say goodbye.

KENNEDY   And only now, the day they take her life,
                    they grant permission she can see her friends.
                    So much has happened, Melvil – but we two
                    can share our stories on another day
                    I didn't want to live this long –

MELVIL   *(Gently.)*   Let's not [make this worse]
                    How is the Queen?

KENNEDY   Composed. And beautiful.
                    She doesn't seem to mourn her life at all.

MELVIL   She is at peace with what is happening?

KENNEDY   You don't let go of living gradually
                    it's one split-second change: it's sudden. Then
                    the mortal world's behind you, and the rest
                    is all eternal. She gave herself to God.
                    And not a word of fear has passed her lips.
                    She only wept when she heard Mortimer
                    had lost his life (and fighting for her cause)
                    she saw his uncle's tears, and wept herself.

MELVIL   Where is she now?

KENNEDY   She prayed most of the night
               sat quietly alone, drew up her will
               and she wrote letters – now she's fast asleep.

Gradually more women arrive, and sit waiting.

MELVIL   Is someone with her?

KENNEDY   Margaret is in there –
               more people have arrived throughout the night.
               It's said they'll set her secretaries free
               the moment she is [dead] –
               And every thing they took – every last jewel
               they've brought them back intact.

MELVIL   Oh these days, these days

Enter MARGARET.

KENNEDY   How is the Queen? Is she awake?

MARGARET   She's dressed.
               She's coming in a moment. Just to say
               she hasn't eaten anything.

KENNEDY nods – sees ALIX about to enter –

MELVIL   She's bringing me the wine.

ALIX, another girl, enters with a single cup of wine, but is weeping –

KENNEDY   Alix? What's wrong?

ALIX   They've built the stage
               I saw it – I was walking past the hall –
               black cloth is thickly hanging down the walls
               a huge dark platform rising from the floor
               a hard block in the centre and a cushion
               and a glinting pearl-grey axe – it's full, the hall
               there's people pushing all around the stage
               waiting –

MELVIL   Shh-shh – she's coming

MARY enters. She is magnificently dressed. She makes an impression on everyone as she arrives among them – things fall quiet. This is star quality, pure and simple – and someone who is about to die.

MARY   Why are we crying? We should all rejoice
                rejoice because our grief is at an end
                my chains all come apart, the prison gates
                lift up – and my pure, joyous soul soars free
                for ever, this time. There's no need to weep.
                We could have wept when under lock and key
                and made to suffer what no queen should suffer
                but now Death is a friend, holds out his hand
                covers my shame with inky wings and offers
                peace. I feel the crown, back on my head.
                The final moment lifts a human up
                no matter who they are or what they've done.
                Is that you, Melvil? Don't kneel down – stand up!
                I'm so happy to see you here – to know
                that you will tell my story once I'm gone,
                a Catholic to witness my last hour.
                But tell me first – what's happened to you all
                since they decided I should be alone?

MELVIL   No – nothing bad has happened – just my rage
                at being so powerless to help your Majesty.

MARY   And how is Didier, my dear old chamberlain?
                He cannot still be with us –

MELVIL   He's alive –
                he's still [alive] –

                ,

MARY   If only I could hold my family
                embrace them one last time, instead
                I'll die with strangers – circling crowds
                and only your tears shed for me. Melvil,
                I bless my Catholic family abroad
                I've written to them all, and to the Pope
                and to the King of France – all in my will

and every gift I give to them is filled
a thousandfold with thanks – however poor.
The King of France will keep you in his care
but please – for my sake – don't stay here in England
don't let them gloat and sing over you all
because you once served me – pack up your things
and quickly leave – today. I want you all to swear –

MELVIL   I swear it – on behalf of everyone

People murmur assent, say 'yes'. The atmosphere is very teary – loving but could break out into sobs at any moment.

MARY   The few possessions I have left, I've shared
among you, if the Queen honours my will –
to my girls – my Alix, Gertrude, Margaret, Rosalind
I leave my pearls – and all my clothes
you're young, you will enjoy them. So, so young.
the clothes I'm wearing now are yours as well.
And Hanna, my faithful, beautiful Hanna
I know you don't want jewels or gold or anything
our memories are our jewels. But still –

MARY has a cloth.

I made you this. Made it for you myself.
My tears are in the stitches. And when it's time
you'll blindfold me with this – fold me into dark
your final service in a history
of matchless duty.

KENNEDY   I don't think I can bear it

MELVIL   Give me a final moment with the Queen

Everyone but MELVIL leaves.

MARY   I stand at the edge of eternity
all my affairs on earth are set in order
You know, I never understood the Protestant faith
setting our own belief above the world
as if the things we see are not God's work.

Humanity is a visible sign itself
we're God's celestial architecture – *here* [on Earth]
The russet of the autumn, and the rise
of some great shimmering butter-yellow tree
laughter in sharp blue eyes – a dragonfly:
all palaces, all signs, written by his hand.
I bid them – and this heavy earth – farewell
I know I go before the Highest Judge
I only wish my God had granted me
a final Catholic service, my last rites.
I'll die without the peace of my own Church.

MELVIL   God can create an altar anywhere –
              and in this prison.

              MELVIL looks at the cup of wine.

MARY   Do you mean – ? Yes – Melvil, yes you do
              There is no priest here – but as our Lord said
              when two of you are gathered in my name
              there am I in the midst of you – Melvil!
              what *makes* a priest? It is something *inside,*
              and with that thing within, you are my priest
              as I am still your queen, despite a world
              that counts us merely as two mortal souls.
              I'll make my last confession now – to you.

MELVIL   You say there's not a priest here – or a church
              but God brings you another miracle.

              MELVIL produces a Host [communion wafer] in a gold case.

              I have received my holy orders – I am a priest
              inside and outside. I bring this for you
              from Rome – and blessed by the Holy Father,
              Communion.

MARY   And once you were my servant. Now you are
              the servant of a greater judge – and throne.
              As you once knelt to me, I kneel to you
              in gratitude. You've brought me happiness.
              Thank you.

MARY kneels.

MELVIL   In the name of the Father, the Son
and the Holy Spirit. Amen.

MARY   Bless me Father, for I have sinned.

MELVIL   What sins weigh on your soul since the last time
you made confession to the God of truth?

MARY   My heart was full of jealous, vengeful hate.
I've prayed to God that He forgives my sins
when I could not forgive my enemy.

MELVIL   Do you repent this sin?

MARY   I do repent.

MELVIL   I'm listening, Mary –

MARY   It wasn't only hate
but love – impulsive, sinful love – my heart –
my heart was always drawn to poisonous men

MELVIL   Do you repent this sin?

MARY   I do repent
it was the hardest fight for me
to let that go. But now the knot's undone.

              ,

I caused a murder once. My husband's death.
I gave myself in marriage to his murderer.
And though I did the penance for the sin
the guilt's still swarming over me – even here,
my last few minutes.

MELVIL   Do you have more to say?

MARY   That's everything. There's nothing else.

MELVIL   Take care
be sure that your confession is complete
leave *nothing* out, offer up every sin
you're near to God now. Seek forgiveness.

MARY   There's nothing I've concealed.

MELVIL   Mary, there is.
            The plots against the English Queen – inciting
            Babington and Parry to their deaths:
            you've not confessed the crimes you're dying for.

MARY   There's nothing I've concealed

MELVIL   So they were lies?
            Your secretaries lied on oath?

MARY   Their judge is God
            I've told the truth. Those crimes were not my crimes.
            I'm ready for eternity – the hand of the clock
            cuts swiftly through my final minutes – and
            I have made my full confession.

MELVIL   You're going to the scaffold innocent?

MARY   This is my penance for my early life.
            My early death redeems my early life.
            God's granting me atonement.

MELVIL   Then may God
            the King, the Father of Mercies,
            who through the death of Jesus Christ Our Lord
            grant you forgiveness – that your frailty
            may not pursue your soul as it finds rest.
            May He pardon your sins.

MARY   Amen. Amen.

MELVIL sees BURLEIGH standing at the door.

The ritual – which would have come to full communion – is interrupted: the cup of wine and the host wait, vulnerable, to one side.

PAULET enters. HANNA and the GIRLS come in, slightly stricken – it's happening now, it seems. The grief, the horror of what is about to happen is unbearable.

BURLEIGH   Lady Stuart, I have come here to confirm
            your last commands.

111

MARY   Lord Burleigh, thank you.
My will contains my wishes – Lord Paulet
you have the document. Please follow it.

PAULET   I will. I swear to you.

MARY   I ask the Queen
to let my people leave England unharmed.
And grant me here my last communion.

BURLEIGH   The Queen will grant you both of these requests.

MARY   And will the Queen allow me burial
on consecrated ground?

BURLEIGH   That cannot be.

MARY   Then let my Hanna take my heart with her,
and bury it, where it has always been –
in France.

BURLEIGH   It shall be done.

MARY   Paulet – come here
give me your hand. I'm sorry for your grief
whatever part I played – unknowingly
in your poor nephew's death, forgive me.
They couldn't break your goodness. Please: I beg
don't hate the memory of me.

PAULET   My lady, God be with you. Go in peace.

One by one, MARY hugs her girls and kisses them –

MARY   My girls, it's time. Come here. Our last goodbyes.
Margaret, your lips are warm! Be kind. Farewell.
Gertrude, goodbye. Don't work too hard, my love.
There's time. For all of you – there's so much time.
My Alix – trust that brain, and trust yourself.
And Rosalind, sweet heart, you'll find the man
the husband that you're dreaming of –
you're going to be loved. I know that's true.
My girls, look up! Material things – on earth

they're traps. Your Queen fell into them. Beware.
No more, now. Girls – *look up!*
They can write that I was hated, but I know
I can call myself loved. I was loved.

LEICESTER has entered, too. Perhaps ELIZABETH too – though she's not literally in the room with everyone else.

BURLEIGH   Do you have / any other –

MARY looks at ELIZABETH.

MARY   Lord Burleigh, tell the Queen I offered my love,
that I was sorry for my violence yesterday
and loved her as a sister – and my heart
in every tiny fibre of its beat
forgave her.
May her reign be a long and happy one.
I wish her luck. In the end, we were the same.

MELVIL has picked up the wine and the host, perhaps.

BURLEIGH   The Dean of our religion waits outside
if you'll allow, he'll bring your soul to God.

MARY   We must be that we are.

A sense now of things coming through their final motions before the finish. History in the making. MARY and HANNA and the WOMEN receive communion from MELVIL, who delivers the service in Latin (if text is needed). MARY is dressed in a simple, clean garment, blessed, and stands barefoot.

MARY   It's come: the time to go. Hanna, my love
walk with me as I take my final steps

BURLEIGH   That's not been authorised

MARY   Would you refuse?
My sister would not let the hands of men
be on my body as I die –

BURLEIGH   The women will *cry*

113

MARY These women will not cry. I promise, sir,
      you underestimate the female sex.
      I *guarantee* you Hanna will not cry.
      Do not divide me from my own true nurse
      she held me as I came into the world
      you'll let her hold me as I leave it

PAULET My lord, allow it

BURLEIGH   Very well

MARY   Now
      I have nothing more in the world. My God,
      as you opened your arms upon the cross
      open them to me

*It's at this moment that she and LEICESTER catch sight of each other.
As she takes those final steps, perhaps there is a sudden, queasy moment
of panic in MARY, she falters, perhaps almost faints and LEICESTER
instinctively catches her. And now the two of them are together.*

MARY looks at LEICESTER.

      You kept your word. You said you'd get me out
      I'm leaving now.

He stands as though annihilated. She speaks in a mild tone.

      It wasn't just my freedom that I wished
      to give to you – I wished you'd make it *worth*
      the years of misery – held up by your love
      I thought we might create a whole new life.
      And now, as the earth falls away from me
      and in the brightening air, I am a spirit,
      now I can tell you – without any shame,
      you conquered me. You really conquered me.
      Leicester. Goodbye. Live happy, if you can.
      You made love to two queens. You made your choice
      you chose the proud heart, not the loving one.
      Kneel down before Elizabeth. I hope
      the loss of me transforms into a profit
      and not a greater loss. For me, on earth
      there's nothing more.

LEICESTER struggles to control himself. He can't speak. The other men look at him: MARY has just confirmed him as part of a plot against ELIZABETH. She's left him no choice but to disappear. Perhaps we hear the noise of the crowds.

MARY walks on, hand in hand with KENNEDY, to her execution.

ELIZABETH is alone. Perhaps a clock ticks somewhere.

'

ELIZABETH   Still no one here. No message. Is it day?
               Does the sun still carve its circle in the sky?
               This waiting is a prison. Is it *done*?
               The day is just a flash inside the night.
               The arrow has been shot – it curves in flight
               it hits the target soon – already – now
               and nothing brings it back.

Enter KENT.

Send Davison in. You're dismissed.

Exit KENT.

I feel such terror I can hardly breathe.
But who can say I did it?
I want to cry for her. I won't know how
to stop –

Enter TALBOT, with urgency.

TALBOT   My Queen, I'm sorry to be here so late
          but there's important news –

ELIZABETH   Go on, my lord

TALBOT   I've had an anxious heart tonight, your Majesty
          so worried for your reputation
          given the Stuart case – and so I went
          to see again the witnesses in the Tower
          the secretaries that testified against
          the Queen, I'm sorry, against Mary Stuart.
          I got there – and my God – they're terrified:

they'd heard the rumour Mary was to die
and fearing heaven's justice more than ours
confessed to me their testimony was *false*.
Those letters were not dictated by the Stuart
the central evidence in Mary's trial
was wrong.

ELIZABETH   They're mad – can they be *trusted*?

TALBOT   Do nothing hastily. We re-open it
examine them again, give her the trial
she should have had before – by English law.

ELIZABETH   We will take your advice. Re-open it.
Though more for your own peace of mind
than fearing reckless judgement from my lords.
There is still time. We must remove all doubt.

Enter DAVISON. KENT waits by the door.

Where is the warrant I left in your hands?

DAVISON   The warrant?

ELIZABETH   The one I gave you yesterday to keep

DAVISON   To keep?

ELIZABETH   I already have a voice. I don't need two.
The people called for me to sign the thing
I did, gave it to you to buy some time
but you know this – and now I want it back.

TALBOT   Davison, we can't lose any time
the legal process has to be re-opened

DAVISON   Re-open?

ELIZABETH   Come *on*. Where is the warrant?

DAVISON   I'm dead.

ELIZABETH   *(Fast.)* Don't tell me that / you –

DAVISON   I don't have it.

116

ELIZABETH How is that [possible]? What?

TALBOT   Christ in Heaven!

DAVISON It is in Burleigh's hands – since yesterday.

ELIZABETH I ordered you to keep it

DAVISON   You did *not* / order me to

ELIZABETH Am I a liar, then? So when did I
tell you to give the death warrant to Burleigh?

DAVISON Not in so many words, Your Majesty, but –

ELIZABETH *'BUT'?* How dare you interpret my words.
Lord Talbot, do you see how my royal name
has been abused

TALBOT   Your Majesty, if he has
without your knowledge, killed a royal queen
he must face formal judgement – if it's done,
your legacy, your history – are mud.

Enter BURLEIGH.

BURLEIGH Long live the Queen – and may your enemies
all perish as your enemy has today.
The Queen of Scots is dead.

                ,

ELIZABETH And did I authorise Queen Mary's death?

BURLEIGH I had the death warrant from Davison

ELIZABETH Did he give you the warrant in *my* name?

BURLEIGH No, he didn't.

ELIZABETH   But you thought that you would
without an order, execute a queen?
Of course, she had been sentenced, and the world
cannot claim that her death was not decreed
but *we know* it was not decreed *by me.*

We have no choice – Burleigh, we banish you
from court – and from our sight. Make no reply.
Dismissed.

BURLEIGH exits. She addresses DAVISON.

Your sentence must be equal to your crime.
You were my secretary. You broke my trust.
For grossly overstepping your authority
you lose your life. They will take you to the Tower.

DAVISON exits. Pale.

,

I should have listened to you from the start,
Lord Talbot, you're the only man I trust
I need you now: my councillor – my friend –

TALBOT   I'm not sure that you'll like my council: it's
'don't banish your best friends'. Honestly, they tried
to serve Your Majesty – as I have, for twelve years
but now you have to set me free – I'm old
too old to bend to these new policies.
Your Majesty, I must resign my office –

ELIZABETH   You cannot leave me now. You saved my life –

TALBOT   Not where it counts. I have saved very little,
I didn't save your better part, my love.
Live long, live happily. Your enemy is dead.
There's nothing more to be afraid of, now.

Exit TALBOT. The room seems huge, empty.

KENT enters.

ELIZABETH   Send in the Earl of Leicester

KENT   Your Majesty
the Earl of Leicester begs to be excused,
he's on a ship to France.

,